Step into a world of **color & beauty** with one of the most celebrated artists of our time, **Barbara Baatz Hillman.**

Barbara's *timeless* floral compositions and detailed depictions of everyday joys have enriched the lives and homes of cross stitchers everywhere. Leisure Arts is proud to present this exciting collection of 20 of Barbara's most popular designs from her years at Kooler Design Studio. Clear photographs show off the *elegance* of the finished pieces, and easy-to-read color charts will have you completing your own natural masterpieces in no time.

barbara baatz hillman

LEISURE ARTS, INC.
Little Rock, Arkansas

staff

EDITORIAL
Vice President and Editor-in-Chief: Sandra Graham Case
Executive Director of Publications: Cheryl Nodine Gunnells
Senior Publications Director: Susan White Sullivan
Special Projects Director: Susan Frantz Wiles
Senior Art Operations Director: Jeff Curtis
Director of Retail Marketing: Stephen Wilson
Director of Designer Relations: Debra Nettles

PRODUCTION
Special Projects Editor: Mary Sullivan Hutcheson
Technical Editor: Carolyn Breeding
Production Assistant: Kathy Elrod
Associate Editor: Kimberly L. Ross

ART
Art Publications Director: Rhonda Hodge Shelby
Art Imaging Director: Mark Hawkins
Art Category Manager: Chaska Richardson Lucas
Lead Production Artist: Karen F. Allbright
Art Production Intern: Autumn Hall
Photography Stylist: Janna B. Laughlin
Staff Photographer: Lloyd Litsey
Publishing Systems Administrator: Becky Riddle
Publishing Systems Assistants: Clint Hanson,
Josh Hyatt, and John Rose

BUSINESS
Chief Operating Officer: Tom Siebenmorgen
Vice President, Sales and Marketing: Pam Stebbins
Director of Sales and Services: Margaret Reinold
Vice President, Operations: Jim Dittrich
Comptroller, Operations: Rob Thieme
Retail Customer Service Manager: Stan Raynor
Print Production Manager: Fred F. Pruss

Some production services provided by **Emerald Ideas, Inc.**

Made in the United States of America.
Softcover ISBN 1-57486-437-8

10   9   8   7   6   5   4   3   2   1

Barbara Baatz Hillman

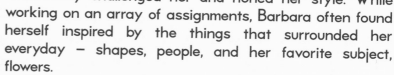

Much like her distinctive designs, Barbara Baatz Hillman's life has been infused with vibrancy and joy.

Art began as a hobby for Barbara — she worked as a school secretary and often painted in her spare time. But the time she invested in oil and acrylic painting soon had Barbara hooked. "I got to where I really enjoyed it, so I quit my job to see how well I could do, artwise."

Taking a chance proved to be a smart move for Barbara. From humble beginnings of featured showings at local malls and area galleries, her gorgeous sense of style caught the eye of market representatives. This exposure became an avenue for Barbara to take her painting to new levels. "From there I began to do cards, note cards, and prints. Companies also hired me as a freelance artist. As jobs came, I just went with them," she shares.

Throughout Barbara's illustrious career, her work has been featured in numerous leaflets, kits, and books, as well as on finished goods, posters, stamps, and quilts. In fact, her talent is so stunning that many are surprised to learn that Barbara is completely self-taught. Possessing no formal training and having no close relatives who were artistic, Barbara says her talent is "just there from somewhere." She remembers that as a child she loved to color, and she developed an interest in needlework as a teenager when she began embroidering pillowcases and working needlepoint designs.

This fascination with needlework continued to blossom when, after working as a freelance artist for several years, Barbara joined the staff of Kooler Design Studio in 1991. She describes her thirteen years at Kooler as "a great experience" that really challenged her and honed her style. While working on an array of assignments, Barbara often found herself inspired by the things that surrounded her everyday — shapes, people, and her favorite subject, flowers.

"There's no end to the design and color potential in flowers," Barbara enthuses. "I like nature more than anything else. It just has so much color, peace, and beauty."

As far as success, Barbara believes that the key is simple — her love for designing is evident in her work. Her greatest hope is that her designs will "give enjoyment to a stitcher or crafter."

In early 2004, Barbara "retired," but she continues to keep busy working as a freelance designer of cross stitch, decorative painting, and quilting patterns. In fact, Barbara may never throw in the towel completely — she describes her long-term plans as "to never stop working on some kind of artistic endeavor."

When she's not designing, Barbara enjoys indulging in some of her favorite pastimes: reading, painting, quilting, traveling, and spending time with her husband and their "very old dog, Bella, and equally old cat, Alex."

contents

amazing grace

10

Chart begins on pg. 32

easter

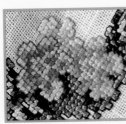

6-7

Charts begin on pg. 22

in the garden

11

Chart begins on pg. 36

floral fancy

8

Chart on pg. 21

token of love

12

Chart begins on pg. 40

our blessing

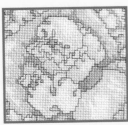

9

Chart begins on pg. 25

grandma's flowers

13

Chart begins on pg. 45

wreath for all seasons

14

Chart begins on pg. 52

beautiful bounty

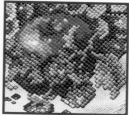

18

Chart begins on pg. 86

morning dew

15

Chart begins on pg. 59

hummingbird banquet

19

Chart begins on pg. 88

stitcher's sampler

16

Chart begins on pg. 72

towels

20

Charts begin on pg. 90

92 alphabets & numbers

watering can collection

17

Chart begins on pg. 79

94 general instructions & finishing

Charts on pg. 22.

The wonder and majesty of **Easter** is beautifully expressed in this assortment of five designs. Brilliantly embellished with Barbara's fresh flowers, two inspiring bookmarks are just right for marking favorite Bible passages. Also featuring a floral motif, the table set consists of a breadcloth, candle band, and table runner...a heavenly collection that will be a vibrant addition to your Easter dinner.

Charts on pgs. 23-24.

Although her current home lacks the space for a large flowerbed, gardening has long been one of Barbara's favorite activities. Her engaging arrangements have been the subject of many a beloved needlework pattern, and Floral Fancy is no exception. A lovely tribute to springtime, this breathtaking design features an assortment of gorgeous blooms proudly displaying their full petals and luxuriant colors. Fashioned into a pillow, this piece promises lasting beauty.

Chart on pg. 21.

The Best of Barbara Baatz Hillman

Nothing is more precious to proud parents and relatives than an angelic newborn baby, a fact that Barbara illustrates perfectly in **Our Blessing**. But there is more to this adorable pattern than simply the unforgettable image — the sleeping babe's clothing was designed to resemble an old-fashioned christening dress, and the dainty patterns found on the tiny pillow and coverlet demonstrate Barbara's appreciation of 'designs within a design.'

Chart on pgs. 25-31.

9

Chart on pgs. 32–35.

With its traditional melody and inspiring lyrics, **Amazing Grace** has stirred the souls of believers for more than 200 years. Written by John Newton, the former servant of a slave trader, the classic hymn is a personal testimony of Newton's later conversion to Christianity and his crusade against slavery. Barbara added her own special touch to this emotive design with a colorful, detailed border and a carefully placed angel.

Based on the 20th chapter of the Gospel of John, this heartwarming hymn was written in 1912 by C. Austin Miles. Asked by a music publisher to compose a tender song that would bring hope to Christians, Miles opened his Bible to this favorite chapter, where he was struck by an image of Mary Magdalene greeting her Savior in the garden after His resurrection. Barbara has adorned **In the Garden** with beautiful, full roses, one of her favorite flowers.

Chart on pgs. 36–39.

11

To love and cherish
from this day
forward

Amanda and Daniel
September 4, 2004

Chart on pgs. 40-44.

The Best of Barbara Baatz Hillman

Crowned by a golden tulip and embellished by a pair of precious cherubs, Token of Love displays a rich, romantic aura. Although it reflects a slightly different style than many of her pieces, Barbara says she had fun creating the exquisite scrollwork and detailed lettering. "It was a different kind of challenge," she confides, adding that she found it "interesting" to create something outside her ordinary design range.

A bouquet of glorious blossoms bends to conceal one of nature's treasures – a tiny nest of fragile blue eggs carefully hidden among a cluster of lush leaves. Barbara says that she chose to color Grandma's Flowers in soft shades of peach, yellow, and sage – more autumnal hues – for artistic variety. An attractive border adds definition and lends an air of natural simplicity.

Chart on pgs. 45-51.

13

Cloaked in an array of seasonal flowers, these beribboned wreaths are bursting with warmth and vitality. From pansies to sunflowers, the four enchanting arrangements are outfitted in the most beautiful blossoms of the four seasons. Barbara carefully selected a variety of birds to add splashes of color to this heartwarming design, Wreath for All Seasons.

Chart on pgs. 52–58.

14

Based on some of Barbara's most treasured memories, Morning Dew is alive with the fresh innocence of dew-kissed hollyhocks. These old-fashioned flowers bring back sweet recollections of Barbara's childhood in Northern California and an expansive garden filled with similar flowers. Barbara confesses that she has a sentimental attachment to these blossoms and is disappointed to see fewer of them in today's gardens.

Chart on pgs. 59-71.

Chart on pgs. 72–78.

The Best of Barbara Baatz Hillman

As a young woman, Barbara developed her sewing skills by making most of her own clothes. Years later, she still sews frequently – although her tastes have turned more to home accessories and quilts. Barbara describes **Stitcher's Sampler** as "a collection of things that I have used or associate with sewing…things that are important to me." This artistic jumble of sewing accessories is sure to delight other seamstresses as well.

From friendly garden creatures to charmingly nostalgic gardening tools, **Watering Can Collection** is a whimsical collage of all the things a nature enthusiast holds dear. Barbara designed this delightful pattern to reflect her love of gardening in general and topiaries in particular. Barbara's fondness for these distinctive trees springs from the creative ways they can be trimmed into an array of shapes – several of which are depicted in this design.

Chart on pgs. 79-85.

17

A curious bird pauses to observe the lush glory of nature's riches. **Beautiful Bounty** was born when Barbara decided that she "wanted to design a fall piece with a lot of color that could be stitched on an afghan or a tablecloth, or be framed." The lifelike dimensions of these harvest fruits demonstrate Barbara's attention to color, texture, and highlights within her artwork.

Chart on pgs. 86-87.

The Best of Barbara Baatz Hillman

Hummingbirds have long been a favorite subject of Barbara's, and she has become adept at capturing the personality and charm of these nimble little birds, as one can see in **Hummingbird Banquet**. Such talent comes in part from observation — one of Barbara's favorite pastimes is watching these graceful winged creatures through a large window in her dining room. In fact, she keeps two feeders full of nectar near the glass to entice them to tarry a while in her yard.

Chart on pgs. 88–89.

Lovely in the guest bath, these **Towels** are also wonderful as gifts! A tassel is a graceful finishing touch for any décor, so what better place to stitch one of the fringed ornaments than on a fingertip towel? Toile is another popular decorative motif, and Barbara designed this delicate pattern with the traditional theme in mind. We provide an alternate color key for the pink version.

Charts on pgs. 90–91.

X	DMC	¼X	B'ST	ANC.	COLOR
•	blanc		◿	2	white
✕	210			108	lt purple
●	309	◿	◿	42	lt red
−	341			117	lt blue
✖	550		◿	102	dk purple
2	552			99	purple
V*	608 &			332 &	
	3340			329	
◒	702			226	dk yellow green
*	704			256	yellow green
★	742			303	dk yellow
O	745			300	yellow
=	772			259	lt yellow green
+	776			24	pink
■	781		◿	309	tan
▲	791		◿	178	dk blue
■	815		◿	43	red

X	DMC	¼X	B'ST	ANC.	COLOR
8	890		◿	218	dk green
•	946			332	dk orange
◉	956			40	dk pink
♥	971			316	yellow orange
H*	3607 &			87 &	
	553			98	
▣	3799	◿	◿	236	grey
✧	3807			122	blue
✚	3815			877	dk blue green
4	3816			876	blue green
$	3817			875	lt blue green
▢	3818			923	green
◇	3824			8	peach
✔	3827			311	lt tan

* Use 2 strands of first color listed and 1 strand
  of second color listed.

Design was stitched on a 13" square of Antique White Cashel Linen® (28 ct). It was stitched over 2 fabric threads. Three strands of floss were used for Cross Stitch and 1 strand for Backstitch. It was made into a pillow.
See Finishing Techniques, page 96.

#1 (30w x 92h)

#2 (28w x 95h)

Designs #1 and #2 were each stitched over 2 fabric threads on an 8" x 13" piece of White Cashel Linen® (28 ct). Three strands of floss were used for Cross Stitch and 1 strand for Backstitch. See Finishing Techniques, page 96.

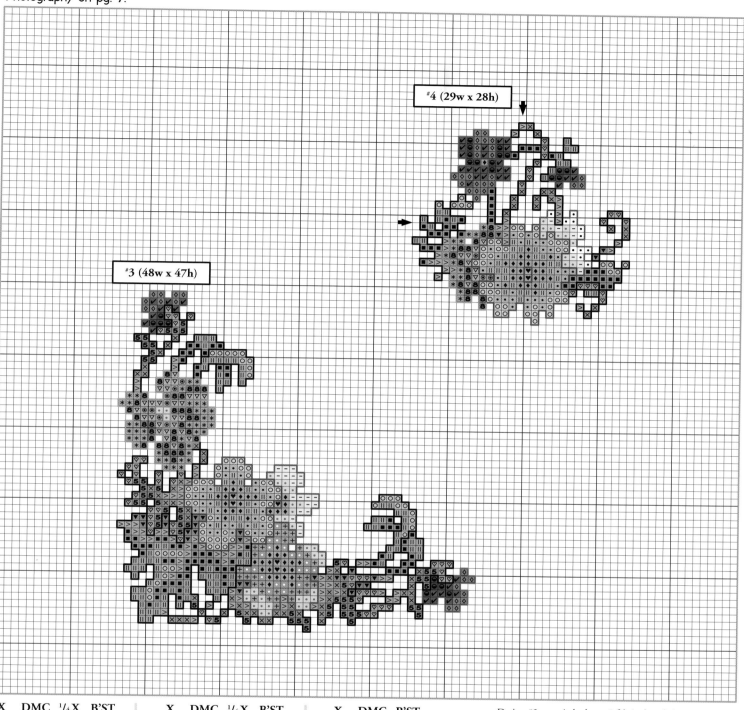

#4 (29w x 28h)

#3 (48w x 47h)

X	DMC	¼X	B'ST
•	blanc		╱ *
✳	210		
‖	309		╱
◇	341		
◉	550		╱
▽	552		
▢ †	608 & 3340		
✕	702		
5	704		
•	742	•	
−	745		
•	747	◢	
♡	772		

X	DMC	¼X	B'ST
⊘	776		
♥	781		╱
⊖	791		╱
★	815		╱
▼	890		╱
⊙	946		
•	956		
•	958		◢
=	959		╱
+	971		
2	3341		
8 †	3607 & 553		
✕	3799		╱ *

X	DMC	B'ST
✔	3807	
☆	3812	╱
▪	3815	
‖	3816	
◎	3817	
＞	3818	
−	3824	
◆	3827	

* For Design #5, use blanc.
  For Design #2, use 3799.

† Use 2 strands of first floss
  color listed and 1 strand
  of second floss color listed.

Design #3 was stitched over 2 fabric threads in one corner of a 19" square of White Cashel Linen® (28 ct) with design 1" from raw edges of fabric. Three strands of floss were used for Cross Stitch and 1 strand for Backstitch. See Finishing Techniques, page 96.

Design #4 was stitched over 2 fabric threads on a 20" x 8" piece of White Cashel Linen® (28 ct). Three strands of floss were used for Cross Stitch and 1 strand for Backstitch. See Finishing Techniques, page 96.

easter

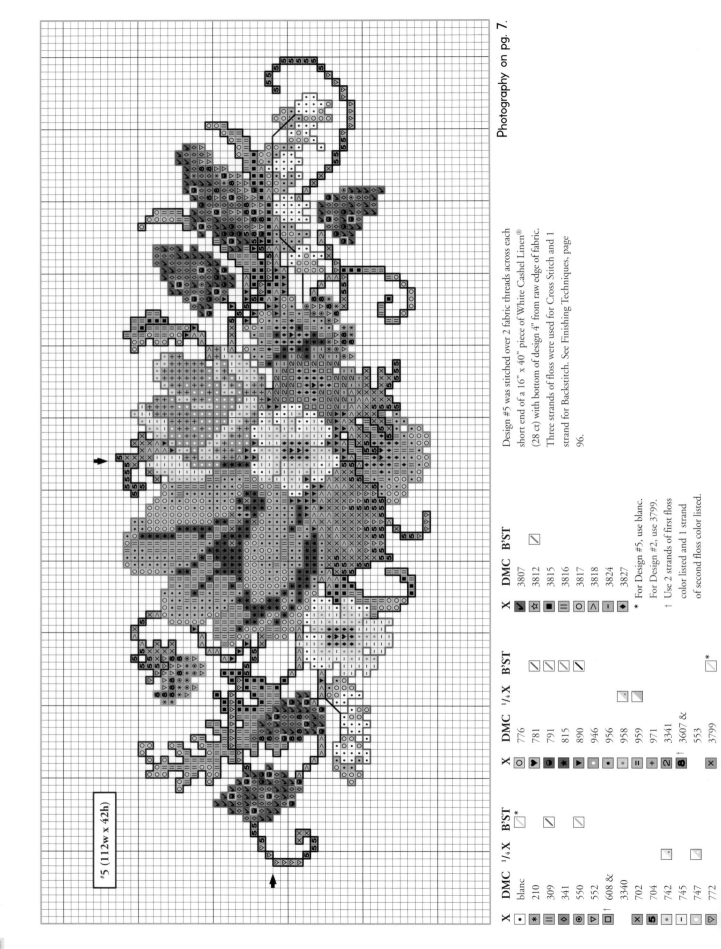

#5 (112w x 42h)

Design #5 was stitched over 2 fabric threads across each short end of a 16" x 40" piece of White Cashel Linen® (28 ct) with bottom of design 4" from raw edge of fabric. Three strands of floss were used for Cross Stitch and 1 strand for Backstitch. See Finishing Techniques, page 96.

X	DMC	¼X	B'ST
•	blanc		*
✳	210		
▤	309		
◇	341		
◉	550		
▷	552		
□	608 &		
	3340		
✕	702		
5	704		
•	742		
I	745	·	
	747		
▷	772		

X	DMC	¼X	B'ST
○	776		
▶	781		
◐	791		
★	815		
▶	890		
▫	946		
•	956		
⊡	958		
‖	959		
+	971		
2	3341		
⊞	3607 & †		
	553		
✕	3799		*

X	DMC	B'ST
◣	3807	◺
☆	3812	
■	3815	
▤	3816	
○	3817	
∧	3818	
-	3824	
◆	3827	

* For Design #5, use blanc. For Design #2, use 3799.
† Use 2 strands of first floss color listed and 1 strand of second floss color listed.

easter

24

The Best of Barbara Baatz Hillman

(Charts on pgs. 26–31. Photography on pg. 9.)

X	DMC	¼X	B'ST	ANC.	COLOR
☆	blanc		╱†	2	white
m*	blanc & 959	m		2 & 186	white & aqua
C*	blanc & 3747			2 & 120	white & lt periwinkle
L	209			109	lavender
a	341	a		117	periwinkle
✓	369			1043	mint green
2	519			1038	blue
6	704			256	yellow green
◇	746			275	yellow
V	747			158	lt blue
	798		╱	131	dk blue
Z	945			881	flesh
I	948	I		1011	lt peach
X	951			1010	lt flesh
3	956		╱	40	coral
	958		╱	187	dk aqua
4	959	4		186	aqua
T	963			73	lt pink
+	964	+		185	lt aqua
	991		╱	1076	vy dk aqua
	3328		╱	1024	peach
	3345		╱	268	green
★	3716			25	pink
8	3756			1037	vy lt blue

▨ Grey areas indicate last row of previous sections of design.

* Use **1** strand of each floss color listed.

† Use long stitches.

Design was stitched on a 15½" x 22" piece of 14 count White Aida (design size 9⅜" x 15⅝"). Two strands of floss were used for Cross Stitch and 1 strand for Backstitch except where noted in key. It was custom framed. Personalize with DMC 798 using alphabets on pg. 92.

Stitch Count (131w x 218h)

14 count	9⅜" x	15⅝"
16 count	8¼" x	13⅝"
18 count	7⅜" x	12⅛"

Placement Diagram

Section 1	Section 2
Section 3	Section 4
Section 5	Section 6

Section I

The Best of Barbara Baatz Hillman

Color key on pg. 25.

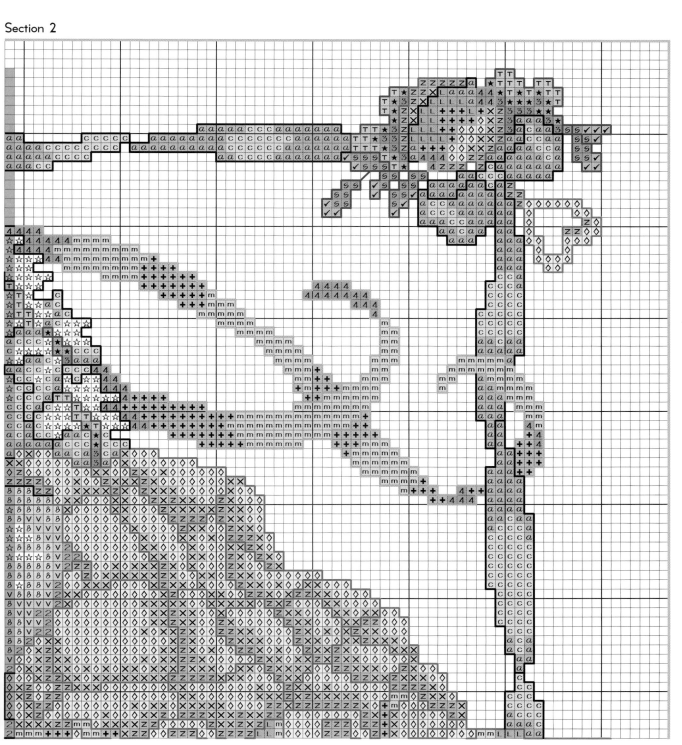

Color key on pg. 25.

our blessing

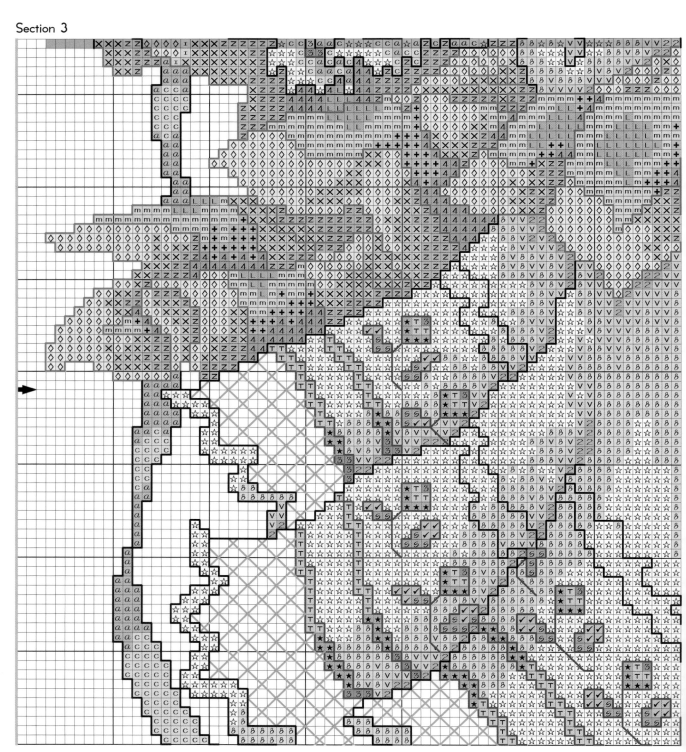

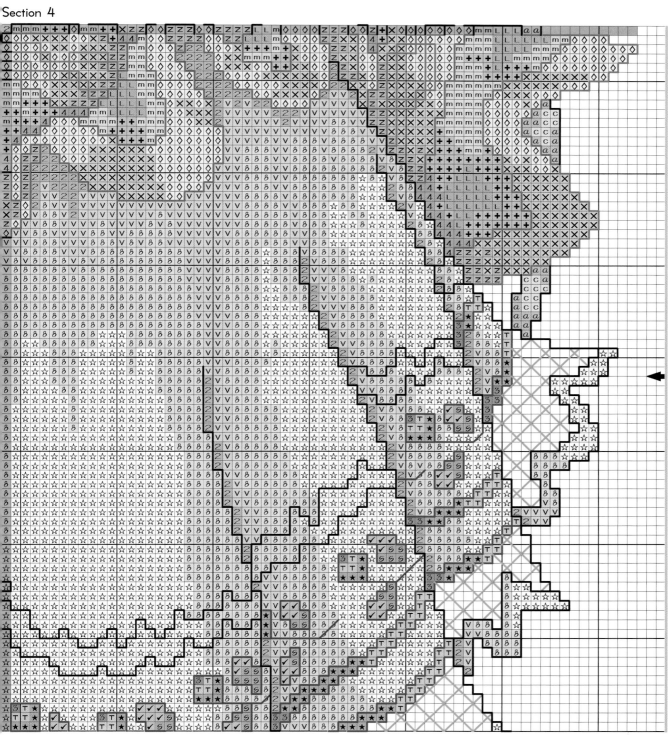

Color key on pg. 25.

our blessing

Born ——————— date ———————

Color key on pg. 25.

our blessing

The Best of Barbara Baatz Hillman

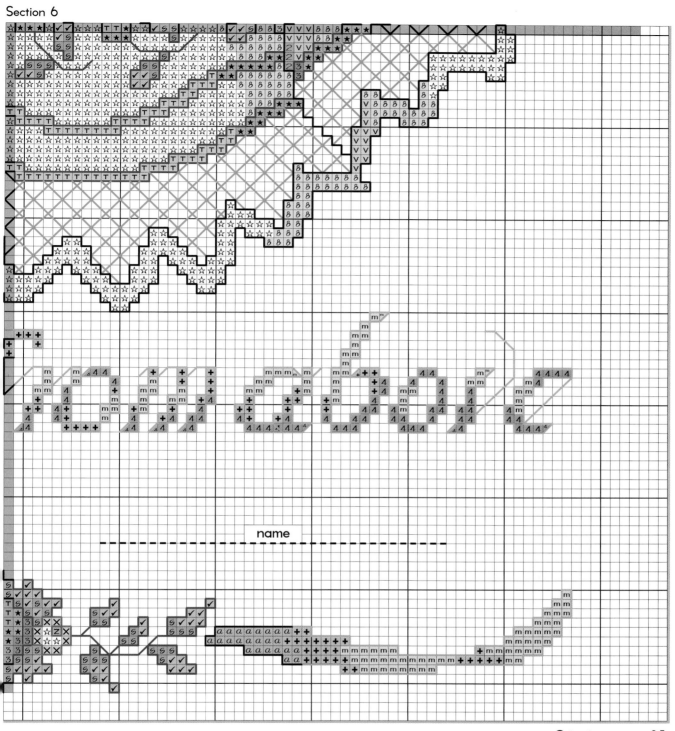

name

Color key on pg. 25.

X	DMC	¼X	B'ST	ANC.		X	DMC	¼X	B'ST	ANC.		X	DMC	¼X	B'ST	ANC.
☆	blanc			2			797		∕	132		◇	3326			36
	309		∕	42		✚	798	◢	∕	131		↑	3350		∕	59
✳	335	◢		38		✔	799	◿		136		✕	3713	◁		1020
★	469		∕*	267		2	809	₂		130		⑤	†002	⑤		
△	471			266		♡	899	◺		52		●	797			132
C	742	c		303		✓	961	◿		76		▨	Grey areas indicate last row			
I	744	ᵢ		301		T	976		∕	1001			of previous sections of design.			

Section I

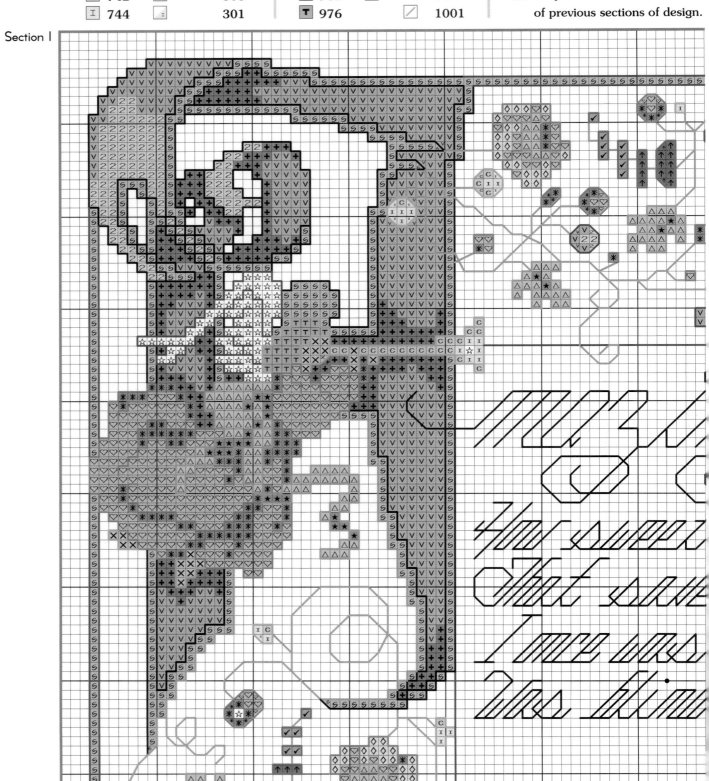

amazing grace

The Best of Barbara Baatz Hillman

* Use **2** strands of floss for stems.

† Use **1** strand of Kreinik Fine (#8) Braid #002 gold.

Design was stitched on a 15¹⁄₂" x 18¹⁄₂" piece of 32 count Antique White Belfast Linen (design size 9¹⁄₄" x 12³⁄₈") over two fabric threads. Two strands of floss were used for Cross Stitch and 1 strand for Backstitch and French Knots except where noted in key. It was custom framed. See Placement Diagram.

Stitch Count (128w x 172h)

14 count	9¹⁄₄"	x	12³⁄₈"
16 count	8"	x	10³⁄₄"
18 count	7¹⁄₈"	x	9⁵⁄₈"

Placement Diagram

SECTION 1	SECTION 2
SECTION 3	SECTION 4

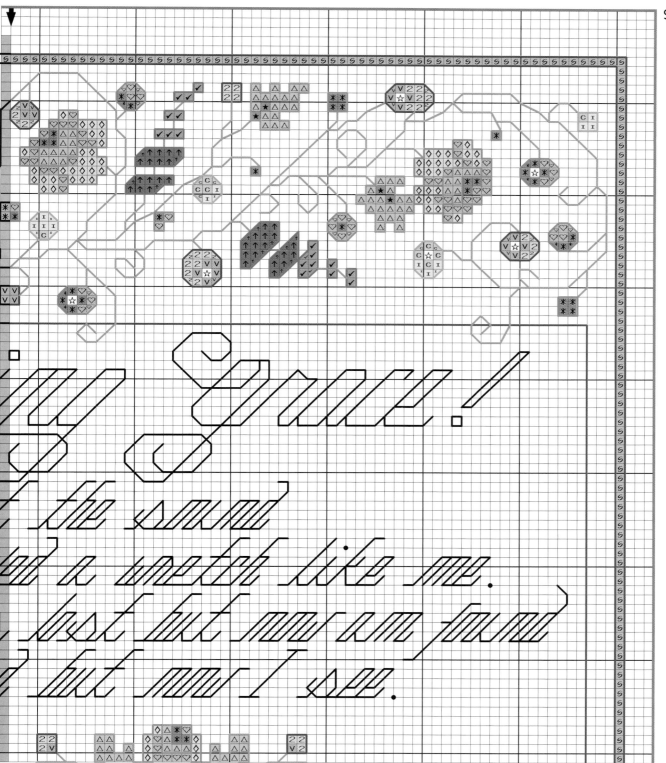

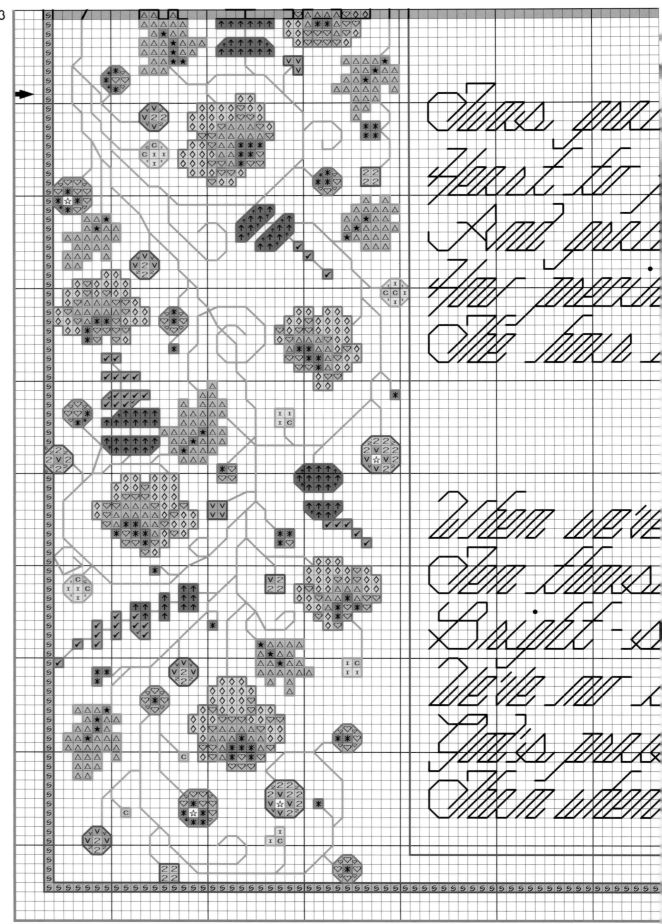

Color key on pg. 32

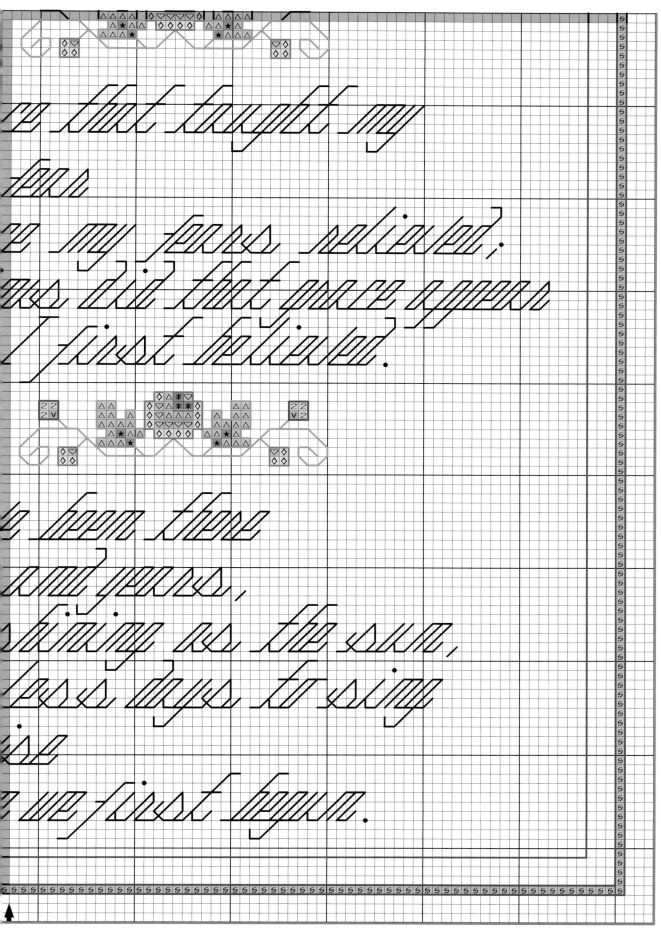

(Charts on pgs. 36–39. Photography on pg. II.)

The Best of Barbara Baatz Hillman

X	DMC	¼X	B'ST
			*
·	blanc		
	309		
	434		
	435		
	503		
	603		
	605		
	742		
	772		
	814		
	818		
	893		
	895		
	898		
	947		
	948		
	959		
	971		
	987		
	989		
	992		
	3340		
	3341		
	3705		
	3708		
	3799		
	3814		
	3824		
	814 Fr. Knot		
	3799 Fr. Knot		
	Grey areas indicate last row of previous sections of design.		

* Use **2** strands of floss.

Design was stitched on a 17½" x 15½" piece of 14 count White Aida (design size 11½" x 9⅛"). Three strands of floss were used for Cross Stitch and 1 strand for Backstitch and French Knots except where noted in key. It was custom framed.

Stitch Count (160w x 127h)

14 count	11½"	x	9⅛"
16 count	10"	x	8"
18 count	9"	x	7⅛"

PLACEMENT DIAGRAM

Section 1	Section 3
Section 2	Section 4

37

X	DMC	1/4X	B'ST
•	blanc		
	309		
	434		
	435		
	503		
	603		
	605		
	742		
	772		
	814		
	818		
	893		
	895		
	898		
	947		
	948		
	959		
	971		
	987		
	989		
	992		
	3340		
	3341		
	3705		
	3708		
	3799		
	3814		
	3824		
	814 Fr. Knot		
	3799 Fr. Knot		

Grey areas indicate
last row of previous
sections of design.
* Use **2** strands of floss.

Section 4

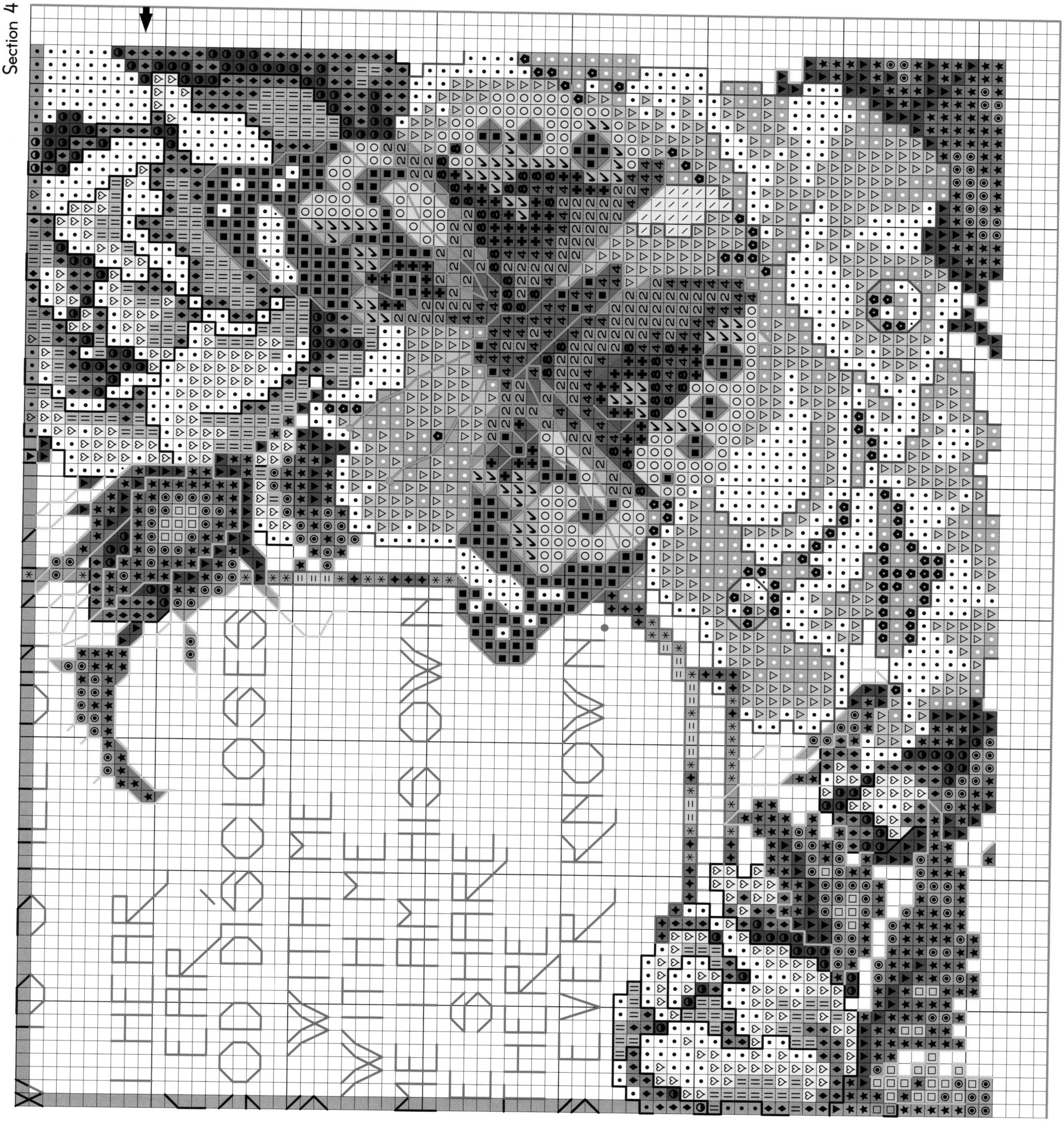

(Charts on pgs. 41-44. Photography on pg. 12.)

X	DMC	1/4X	B'ST	ANC.	COLOR
☆	blanc		⟋*	2	white
◤	209			109	lavender
⊡	211			342	lt lavender
◗	310			403	black
◉	321			9046	red
▲	322			978	blue
◣	350			11	vy dk peach
✳	351			10	dk peach
L	352			9	peach
7	472			253	lt green
	535		⟋	401	grey
Z	680			901	gold
✕	726			295	dk yellow
H	729			890	lt gold
◖	742			303	vy dk yellow
◇	744			301	yellow
+	754	+		1012	lt peach
✚	816			1005	dk red

X	DMC	B'ST	ANC.	COLOR
⊥	827		160	lt blue
~	892		33	coral
a	921	⟋	1003	copper
∧	948		1011	vy lt peach
△	957		50	lt coral
⟋	963		73	pink
V	971		316	orange
◆	986		246	dk green
S	3078		292	lt yellow
↑	3347		266	green
✓	3608		86	fuchsia
4	3761		928	lt turquoise
m	3766		167	turquoise
●	Mill Hill Seed Beads #00479 white			
▨	Grey areas indicate last row of previous sections of design.			

*Use long stitches.

Note: Personalize with DMC 535 using alphabet and numbers on pg. 93.

Design was stitched on a 15" x 17½" piece of 14 count Antique White Aida (design size 8⅝" x 11¼"). Two strands of floss were used for Cross Stitch and 1 strand for Backstitch. It was custom framed. See Placement Diagram.

Stitch Count (120w x 156h)

14 count	8⅝"	x	11¼"
16 count	7½"	x	9¾"
18 count	6¾"	x	8¾"

Placement Diagram

SECTION 1	SECTION 2
SECTION 3	SECTION 4

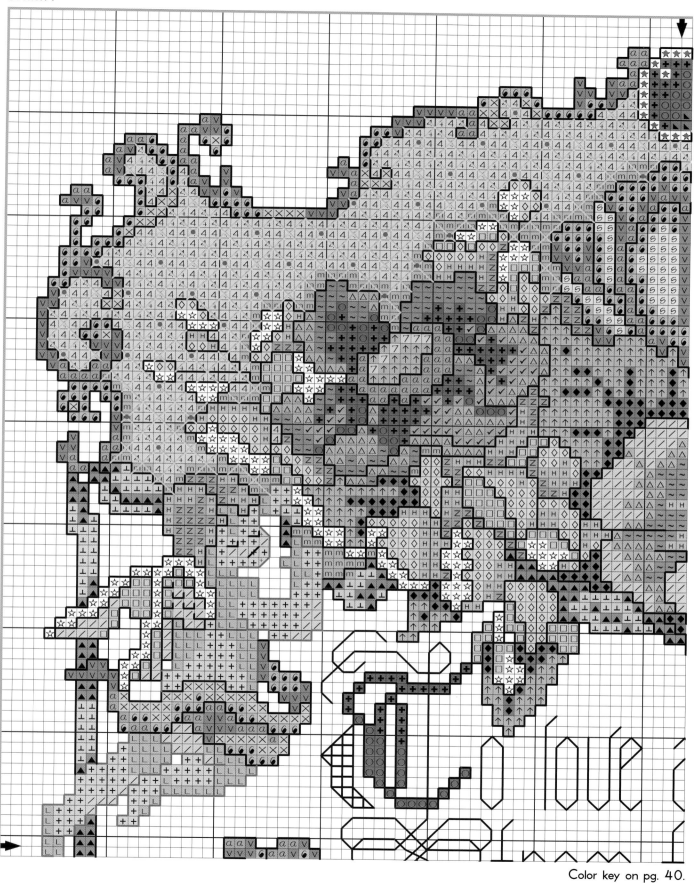

Color key on pg. 40.

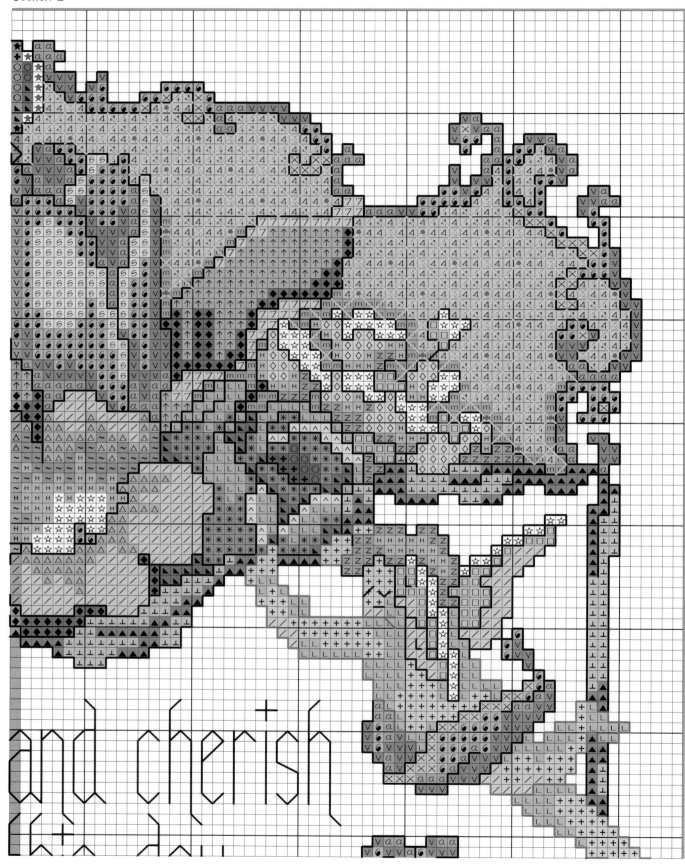

Color key on pg. 40.

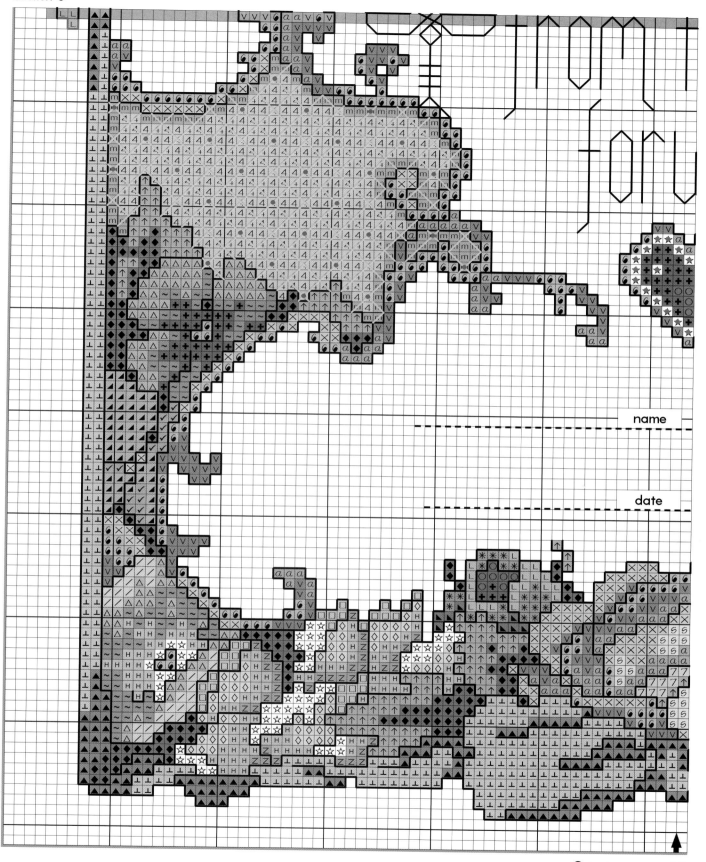

name

date

Color key on pg. 40.

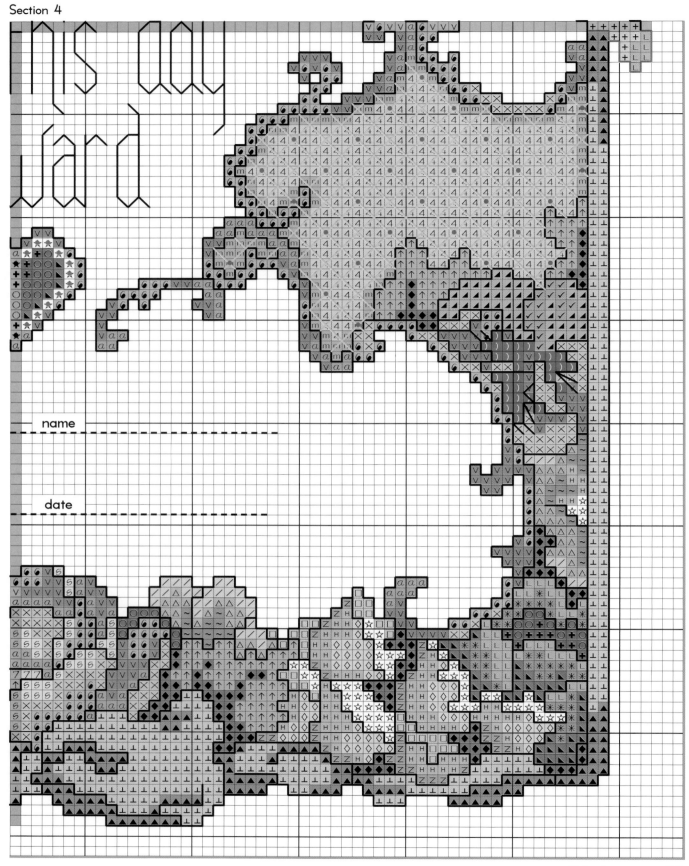

name

date

Color key on pg. 40.

(Charts on pgs. 46-51. Photography on pg. 13.)

X	DMC	1/4X	B'ST	ANC.	COLOR
☆	blanc	☆		2	white
¢	209			109	lt purple
★	301		/	1049	dk copper
◆◆	321			9046	red
✚	350			11	dk peach
V	352			9	peach
5	471			266	lt green
a	500		/	683	dk blue green
L	501			878	blue green
8	502			877	lt blue green
∧	504			1042	vy lt blue green
▬	550		/	102	dk purple
✳	552			99	purple
S	604	6		55	pink
2	745	2		300	yellow
n	772			259	vy lt green
z	807			168	aqua
♡	816		/	1005	dk red
↑	839			1086	dk brown
◇	917	ø		89	fuchsia
✚	939		/	152	navy blue
⊥	956			40	coral
▷	963			73	lt pink
$	3012			844	olive
∾	3013	∾		842	lt olive
♠	3051	♠		681	dk olive
▲	3345			268	dk green
>	3347			266	green
C	3371		/	382	vy dk brown
4	3607	4		87	lt fuchsia
L	3765			170	dk aqua
√	3766			167	lt aqua
e	3776			1048	copper
m	3824			8	lt peach
✕	3827			311	lt copper
6	3863	6		379	brown
T	3864			376	lt brown
●	745			300	yellow Fr. Knot

▨ Grey areas indicate last row of previous sections of design.

Design was stitched on a 17½" x 20" piece of 14 count White Aida (design size 11½" x 13¾"). Two strands of floss were used for Cross Stitch and 1 strand for Backstitch and French Knots. See Placement Diagram.

Stitch Count (160w x 192h)

14 count	11½"	x	13¾"
16 count	10"	x	12"
18 count	9"	x	10¾"

Placement Diagram

SECTION 1	SECTION 2
SECTION 3	SECTION 4
SECTION 5	SECTION 6

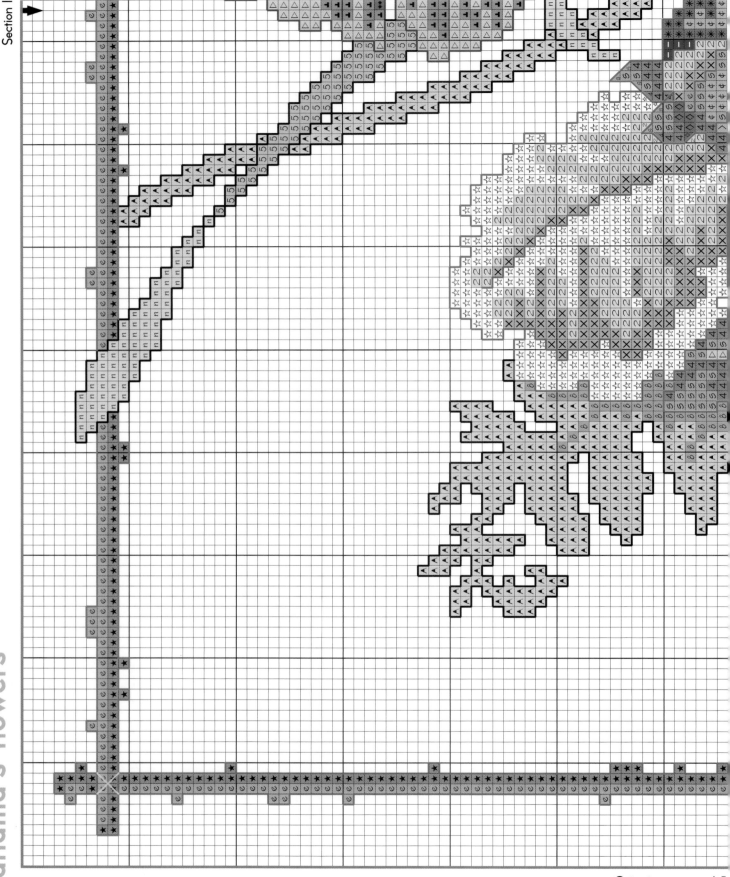

Color key on pg. 45

Color key on pg. 45.

Color key on pg. 4.

The Best of Barbara Baatz Hillman

Color key on pg. 45.

Color key on pg. 4:

The Best of Barbara Baatz Hillman

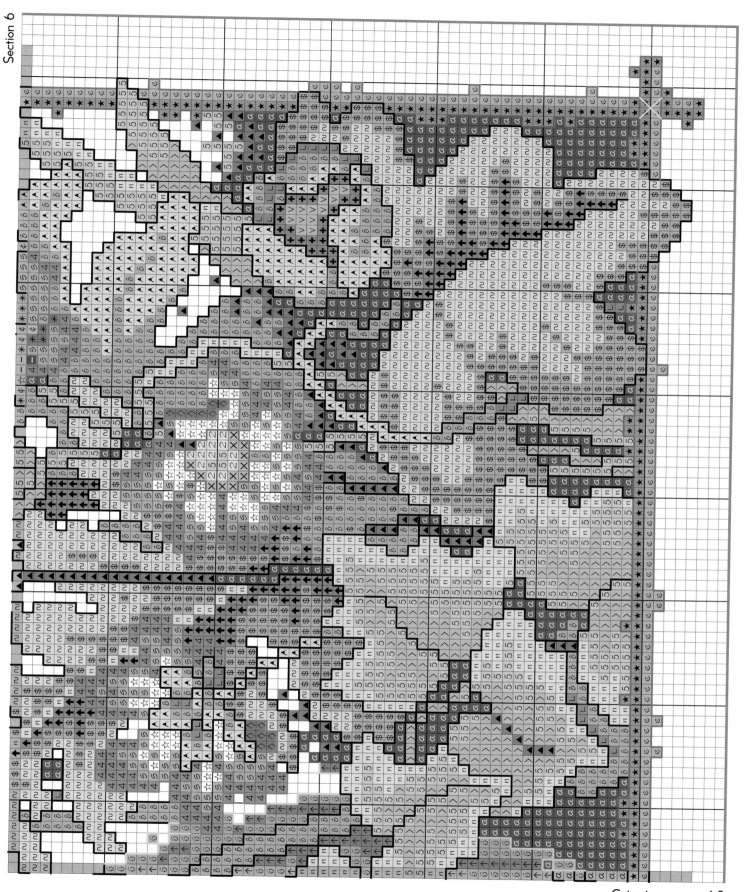

Color key on pg. 45.

(Charts on pgs. 53–58. Photography on pg. 14.)

X	DMC	1/4X	B'ST	ANC.	COLOR
☆	blanc			2	white
C	210			108	lavender
◗	310	◗	╱	403	black
▲	333		╱	119	purple
6 *	415 &	6		398 &	grey &
	3072			847	beige
◆◆	437			362	tan
L	445	L		288	yellow
V	606	V		334	lt red
✚	610	✚	╱	889	brown
I	612			832	lt brown
✛	666	✛		46	red
3	699	3	╱†	923	dk green
╱	701			227	green
−	703	−		238	lt green
▼	725			305	dk yellow
‹	739	‹		387	lt tan
8	741	8		304	orange
%	742	%		303	lt orange
H	747	H		158	lt aqua
◇	772			259	lt mint green
$	813	$		161	lt blue
✕	816	✕	╱	1005	dk red
4	826	4	╱	161	blue
›	927	›		848	blue grey
7	947			330	dk orange
e	956			40	dk coral
♡	957			50	coral
⊥	963			73	lt coral
5	989			242	mint green
n	3078			292	lt yellow
=	3607			87	fuchsia
√	3608			86	lt fuchsia
2	3766			167	aqua
●	blanc			2	white Fr. Knot

▨ Grey areas indicate last row of previous sections of design.

*Use **1** strand of each floss color listed.

†Use long stitches for needles in winter wreath.

Design was stitched on a 19" x 18½" piece of 14 count Antique White Aida (design size 12¾" x 12¼"). Two strands of floss were used for Cross Stitch, 1 strand for Backstitch, and 3 strands for French Knots. See Placement Diagram.

Stitch Count (177w x 170h)

14 count	12¾"	x 12¼"
16 count	11⅛"	x 10⅝"
18 count	9⅞"	x 9½"

Placement Diagram

SECTION 1	SECTION 2	SECTION 3
SECTION 4	SECTION 5	SECTION 6

wreath for all seasons

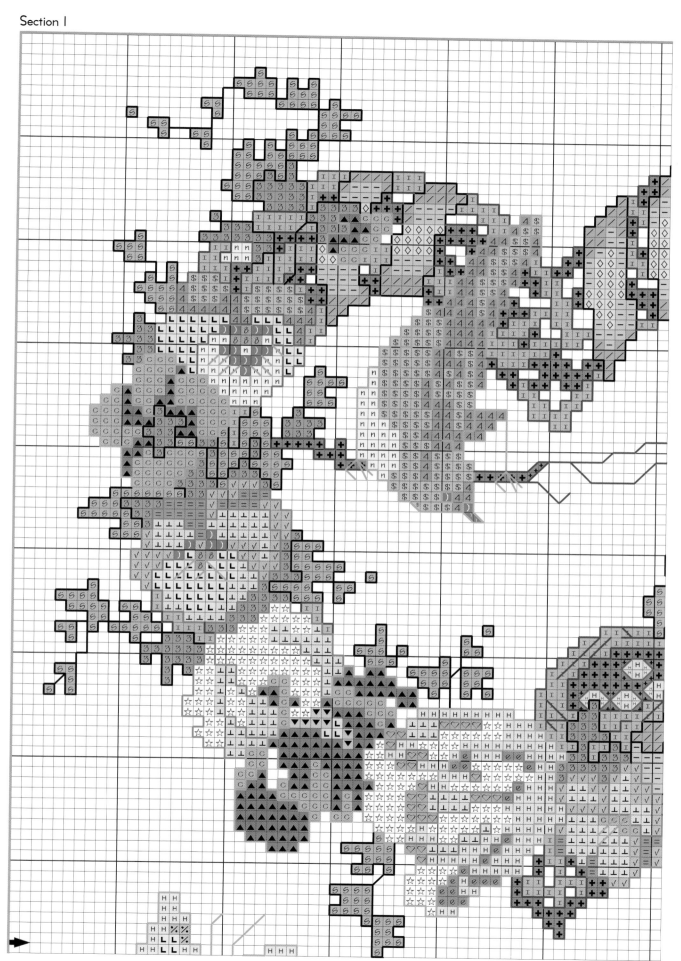

Color key on pg. 52.

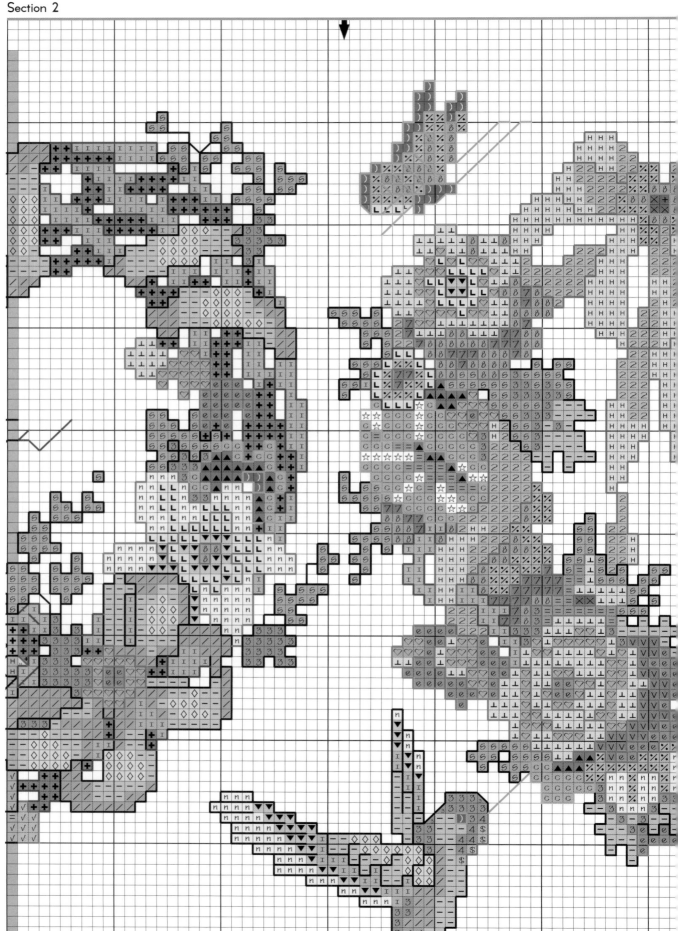

wreath for all seasons

The Best of Barbara Baatz Hillman

Color key on pg. 52

Color key on pg. 52.

Color key on pg. 52.

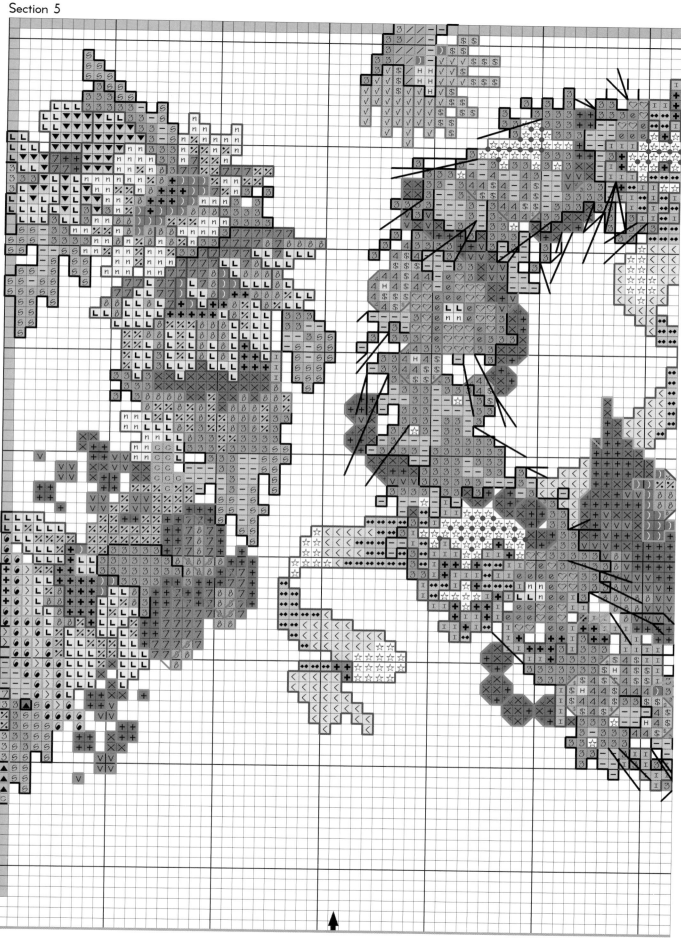

The Best of Barbara Baatz Hillman

Color key on pg. 52.

wreath for all seasons

(Charts on pgs. 60–71. Photography on pg. 15.)

X	DMC	¼X	B'ST	ANC.	COLOR
☆	blanc	☑		2	white
~	*blanc &	-		2	white &
	032				pearl
n	209			109	lt purple
⊥	300		☑	352	dk copper
)	310	◢	☑	403	black
♥	321	◢		9046	lt red
₵	*321 &			9046	lt red &
	003				red
✕	327			100	purple
▷	†327 &	◢		100 &	purple &
	917			89	fuchsia
⊥	340			118	violet
7	341			117	lt violet
m	369			1043	mint green
V	500		☑	683	dk blue green
Z	501			878	blue green
T	502			877	lt blue green
√	504			1042	vy lt blue green
a	550	◢	☑	102	dk purple
4	†601 &			57 &	dk pink &
	3607			87	lt fuchsia
∧	604	◢		55	pink
2	605	◢		1094	lt pink
▲	699			923	dk green
△	702	◢		226	green
e	704	◢		256	lt green
↑	744	↑		301	yellow
◈	814		☑	45	dk red
n	816	◢	☑	1005	red
+	818			23	vy lt pink
–	956	◢		40	coral
5	986			246	dk yellow green
✱	989			242	lt yellow green
▶	3012			844	olive green
Y	3013			842	lt olive green
▢	3051			681	dk olive green
L	3346			267	yellow green
8	3756			1037	blue
C	3806	◢		62	vy dk pink
H	3826			1049	copper
★	3854	◢		313	lt copper

▨ Grey areas indicate last row of previous sections of design.

*Use **1** strand of floss and **1** strand of Kreinik
Balger® Blending Filament.
†Use **1** strand of each floss color listed.

Design was stitched on a 23½" x 24" piece of 14 count Ivory Aida (design size 17½" x 17¾"). Two strands of floss were used for Cross Stitch and 1 strand for Backstitch except where noted in key. See Placement Diagram.

Stitch Count (245w x 248h)

14 count	17½"	x	17¾"
16 count	15⅜"	x	15½"
18 count	13⅝"	x	13⅞"

Placement Diagram

SECTION 1	SECTION 2	SECTION 3	SECTION 4
SECTION 5	SECTION 6	SECTION 7	SECTION 8
SECTION 9	SECTION 10	SECTION 11	SECTION 12

morning dew

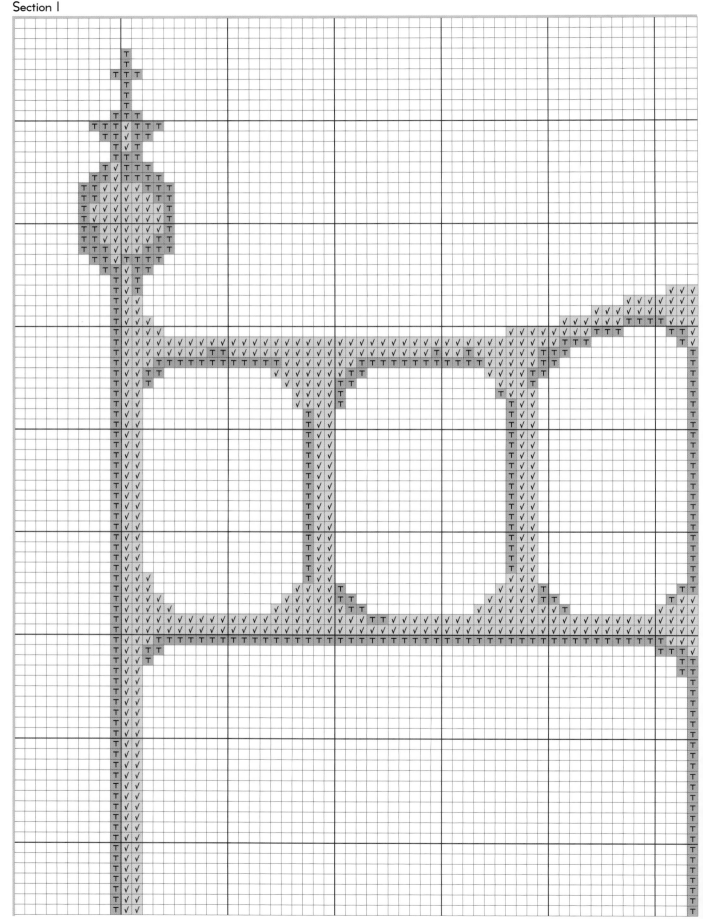

Color key on pg. 59.

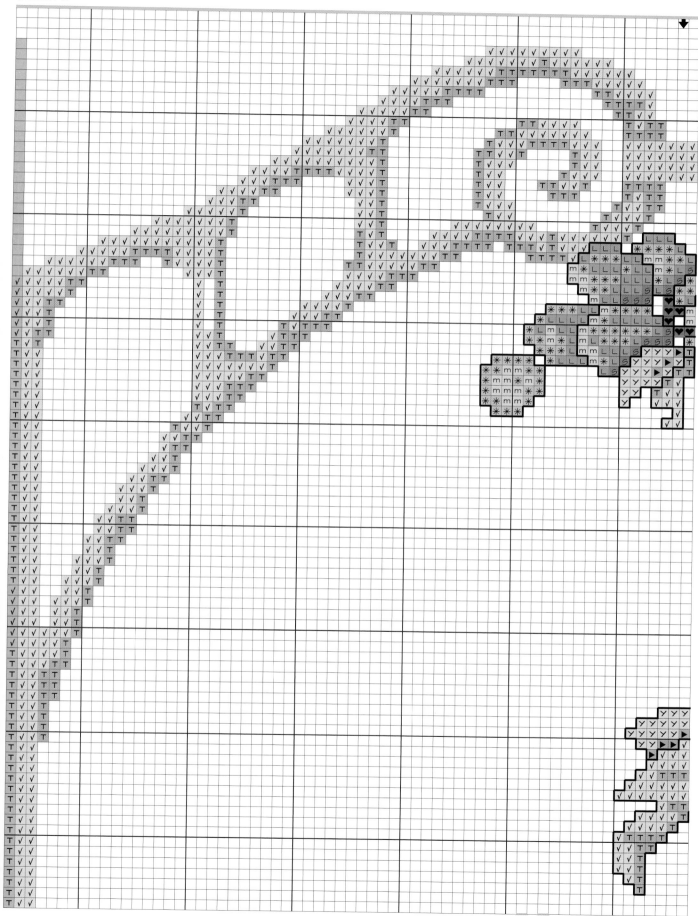

Color key on pg. 59.

Color key on pg. 59.

morning dew

Color key on pg. 59

The Best of Barbara Baatz Hillman

Color key on pg. 59.

Color key on pg. 59

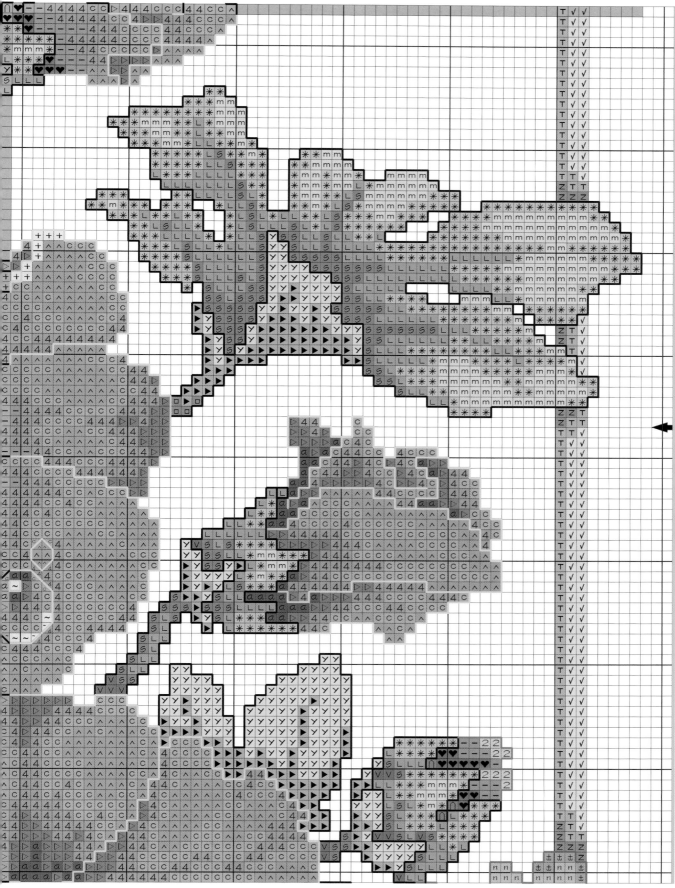

Color key on pg. 59.

Color key on pg. 59.

Color key on pg. 59.

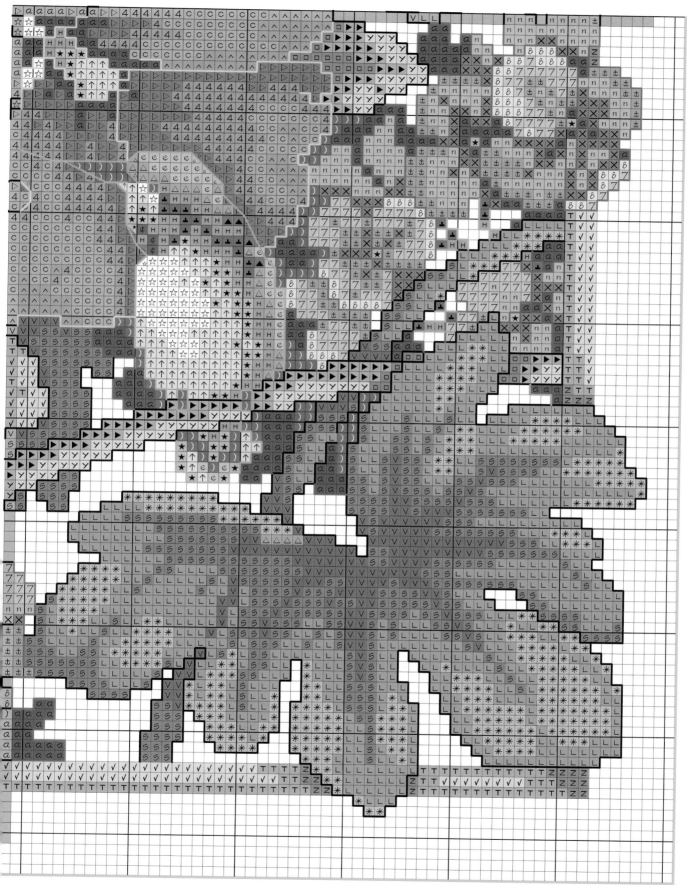

Color key on pg. 59.

(Charts on pgs. 73–78. Photography on pg. 16.)

X	DMC	¼X	B'ST	ANC.	COLOR
☆	blanc			2	white
∩	208			110	dk lavender
=	209			109	lavender
L	211		╱	342	lt lavender
)	310		╱	403	black
♡	333			119	purple
n	341			117	lt blue
♥	350		╱	11	dk peach
8	352			9	peach
−	369			1043	lt green
★	413	◢	╱*	236	dk grey
¢	414	◢		235	grey
↑	415	◢		398	lt grey
▼	517	◢		162	dk turquoise
V	721	◢		925	orange
★	742	◢		303	dk yellow
Y	746			275	lt yellow
╱	747			158	lt turquoise
O	781	◢		308	gold
Z	783	◢		306	lt gold
◆	792		╱†	941	dk blue
+	793			176	blue
L	920			1004	rust
+	948			1011	vy lt peach
△	964			185	lt aqua
S	989			242	green
✕	991			1076	dk aqua
2	992		╱	1072	aqua
T	3024			397	beige
√	3345			268	dk green
✳	3766	◢		167	turquoise
C	3824			8	lt peach
∧	3855	◢		311	yellow

▨ Grey areas indicate last row of previous sections of design.

*Use long stitches for straight pins and needles.

†Use long stitches for sewing machine thread.

Note: Personalize using DMC 792 and alphabets on pg. 92.

Design was stitched on a 14" x 20" piece of 14 count White Aida (design size 8" x 14"). Two strands of floss were used for Cross Stitch and 1 strand for Backstitch. It was custom framed. See Placement Diagram.

Stitch Count (112w x 196h)

14 count	8"	x	14"
16 count	7"	x	12¼"
18 count	6¼"	x	11"

Placement Diagram

SECTION 1	SECTION 2
SECTION 3	SECTION 4
SECTION 5	SECTION 6

stitcher's sampler

The Best of Barbara Baatz Hillman

Color key on pg. 72.

Color key on pg. 72.

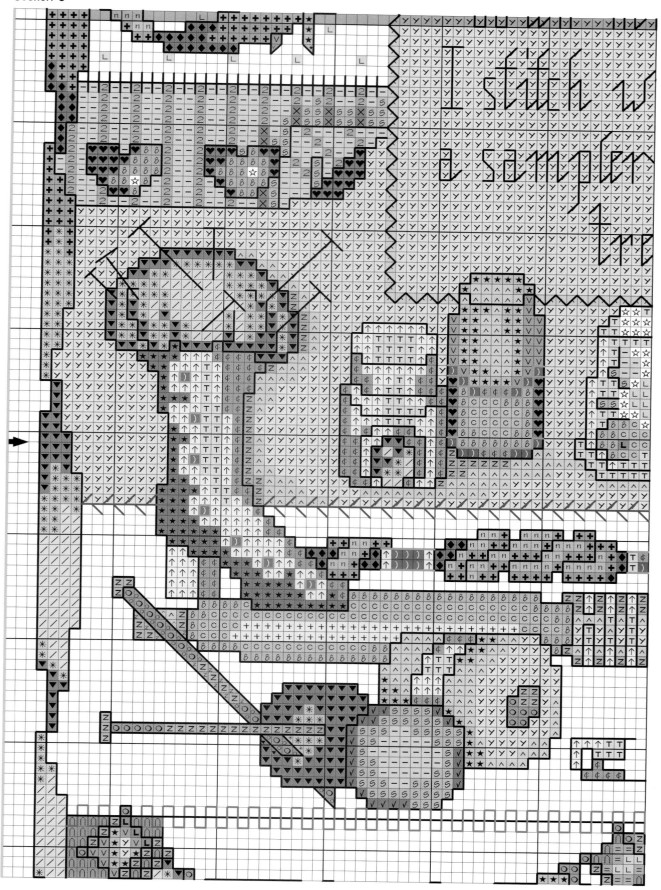

Color key on pg. 72.

Color key on pg. 72.

The Best of Barbara Baatz Hillman

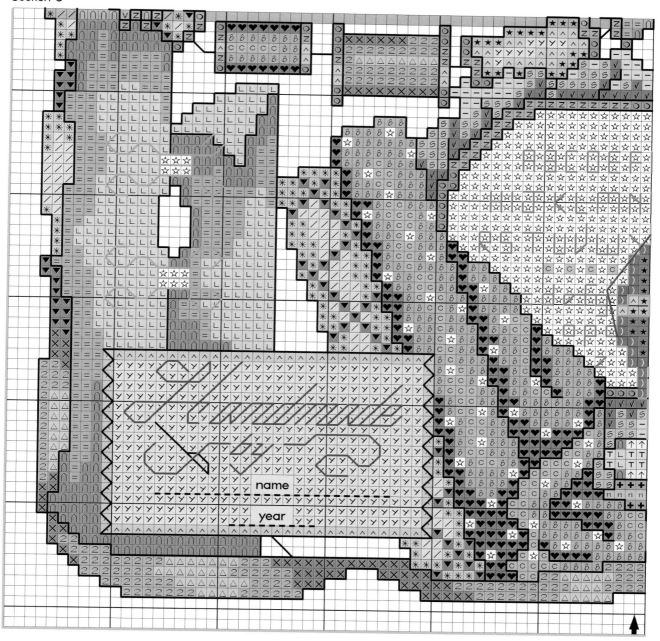

name

year

Color key on pg. 72.

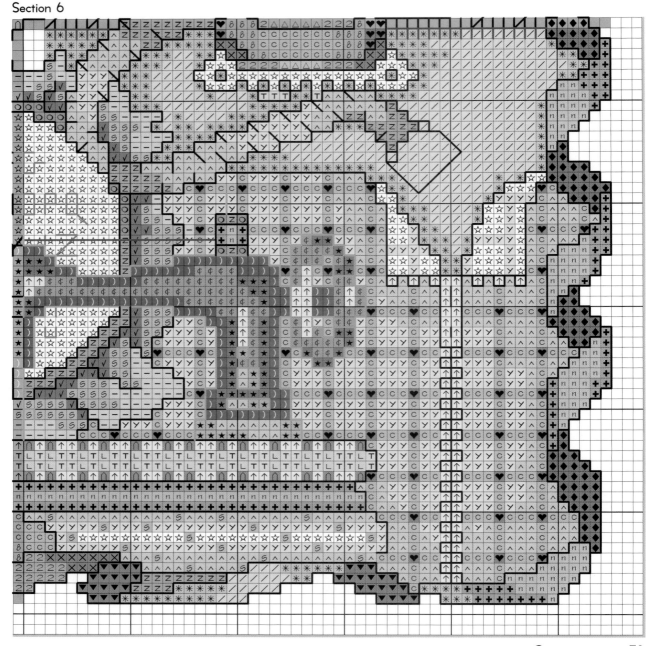

Color key on pg. 72.

(Charts on pgs. 80-85. Photography on pg. 17.)

X	DMC	1/4X	1/2X	B'ST	ANC.	COLOR
☆	blanc	☆			2	white
✓	ecru	✓			387	ecru
✳	209	✳			109	lavender
V	211		♡		342	lt lavender
◄	301	◄			1049	dk copper
▬	319			╱	218	dk green
6	327	6		╱	100	dk lavender
4	334	4		╱	977	blue
△	352	△			9	peach
H	413	H			236	dk grey
5	414	5			235	grey
8	519	8			1038	lt blue
a	642	a			392	taupe
◇	646	◇			8581	dk taupe
L	704	L			256	yellow green
∩	743	∩			302	yellow
~	745	~			300	lt yellow
↑	762	↑			234	lt grey
S	772	S			259	mint green
C	797	C		╱	132	dk blue
=	919	=		╱	340	rust
×	964	×			185	lt aqua
∧	991	∧			1076	dk aqua
3	992	3			1072	aqua
T	3033	T			391	lt taupe
✚	3328	✚			1024	dk peach
▷	3346	▷			267	green
2	3776	2			1048	copper
e	3799	e		╱	236	vy dk grey
Y	3824	Y			8	lt peach
7	3854	7		╱*	313	lt copper
●	blanc				2	white Fr. Knot
●	3799				236	vy dk grey Fr. Knot

▨ Grey areas indicate last row of previous sections of design.

*Use **2** strands of floss and long stitches.

Design was stitched on a 17½" x 20½" piece of 14 count White Aida (design size 11⅛" x 14⅛"). Two strands of floss were used for Cross Stitch and 1 strand for Half Cross Stitch, Backstitch, and French Knots except where noted in key. See Placement Diagram.

Stitch Count (155w x 197h)

14 count	11⅛"	x 14⅛"
16 count	9¾"	x 12⅜"
18 count	8⅝"	x 11"

Placement Diagram

SECTION 1	SECTION 4
SECTION 2	SECTION 5
SECTION 3	SECTION 6

watering can collection

Section I

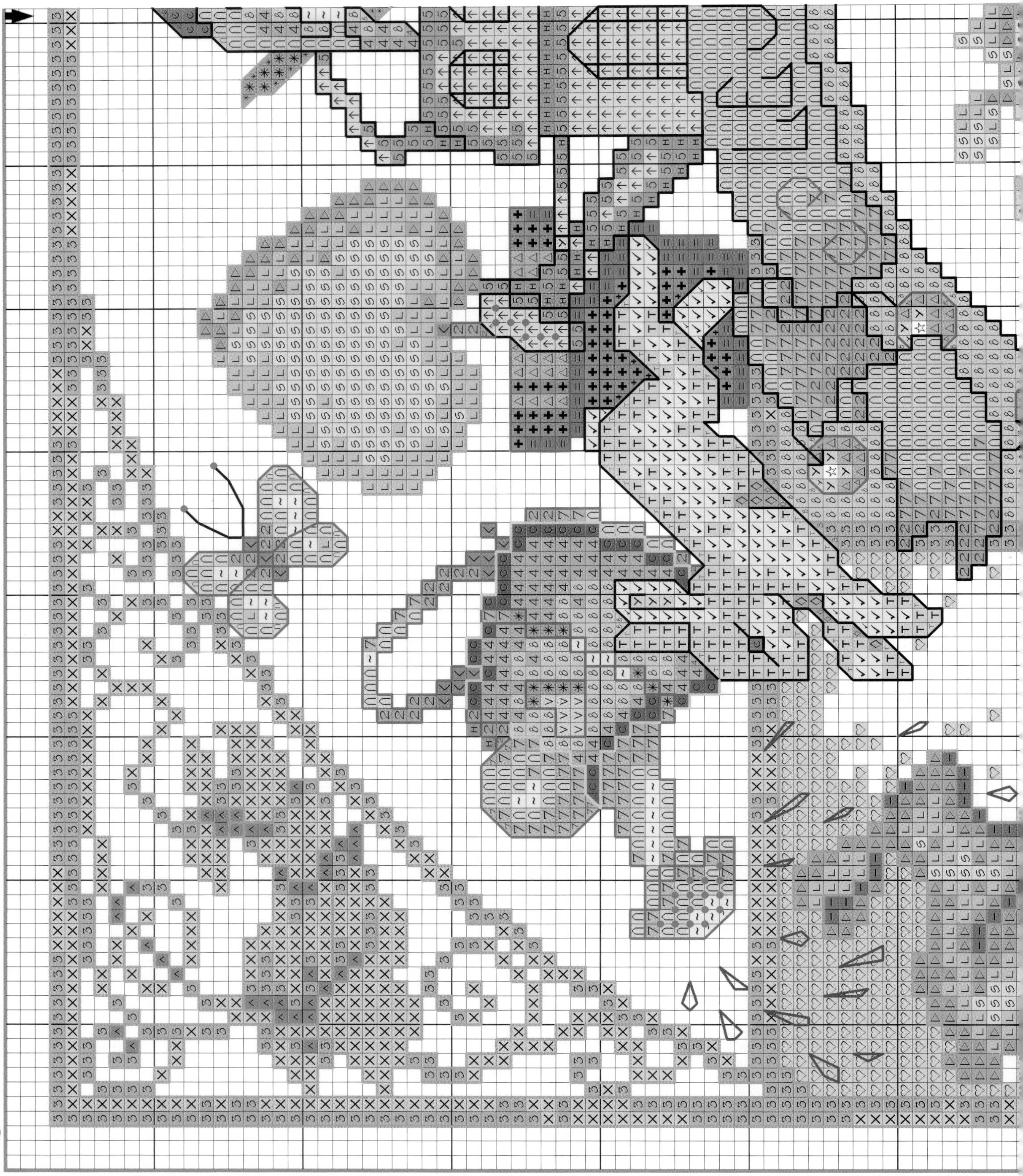

Color key on pg. 7

Color key on pg. 79.

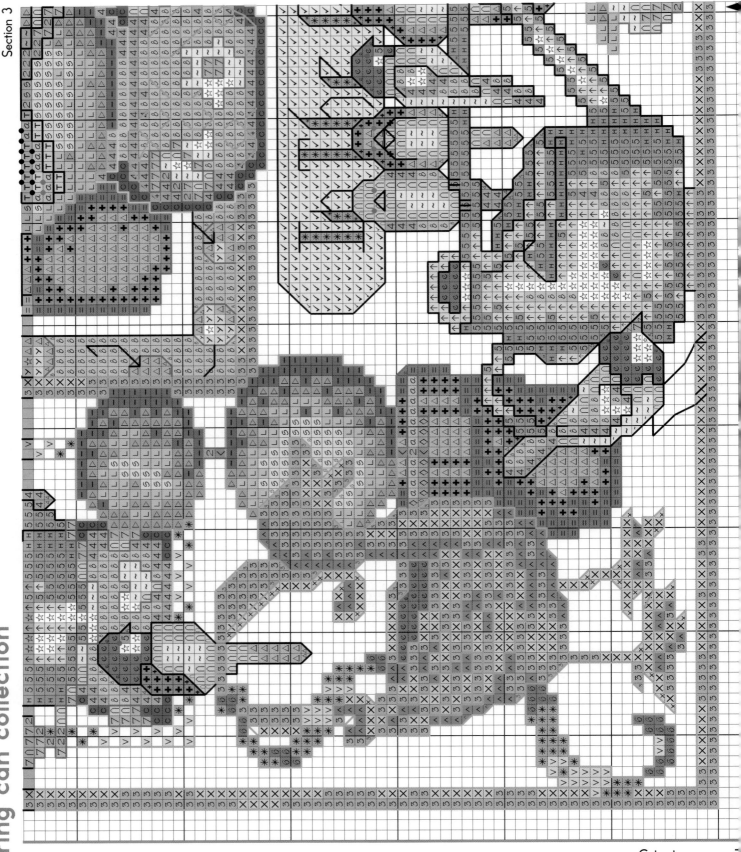

Color key on pg. 7

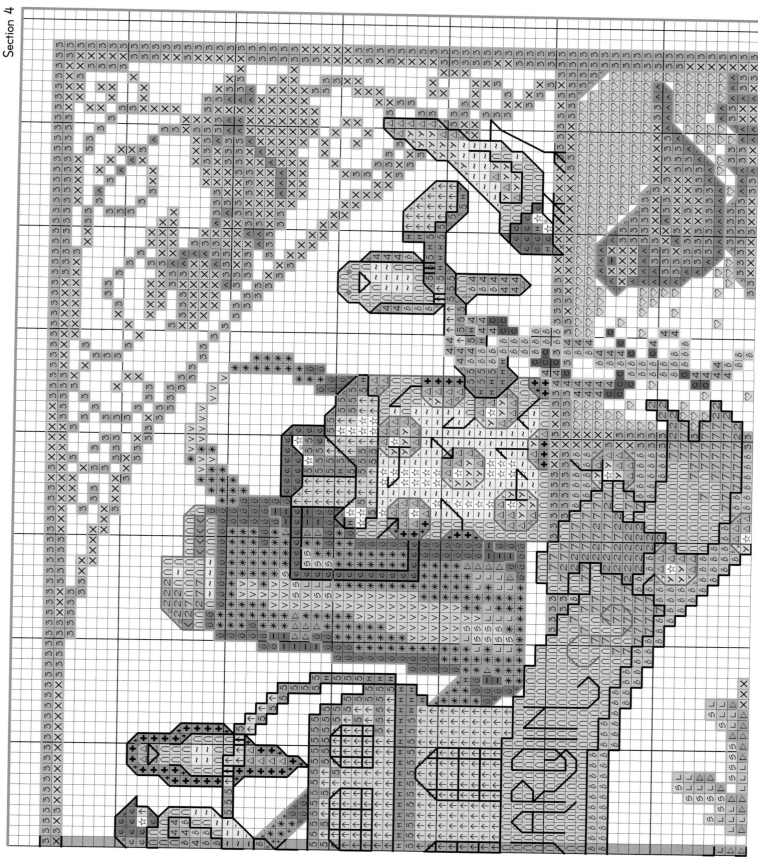

Color key on pg. 79.

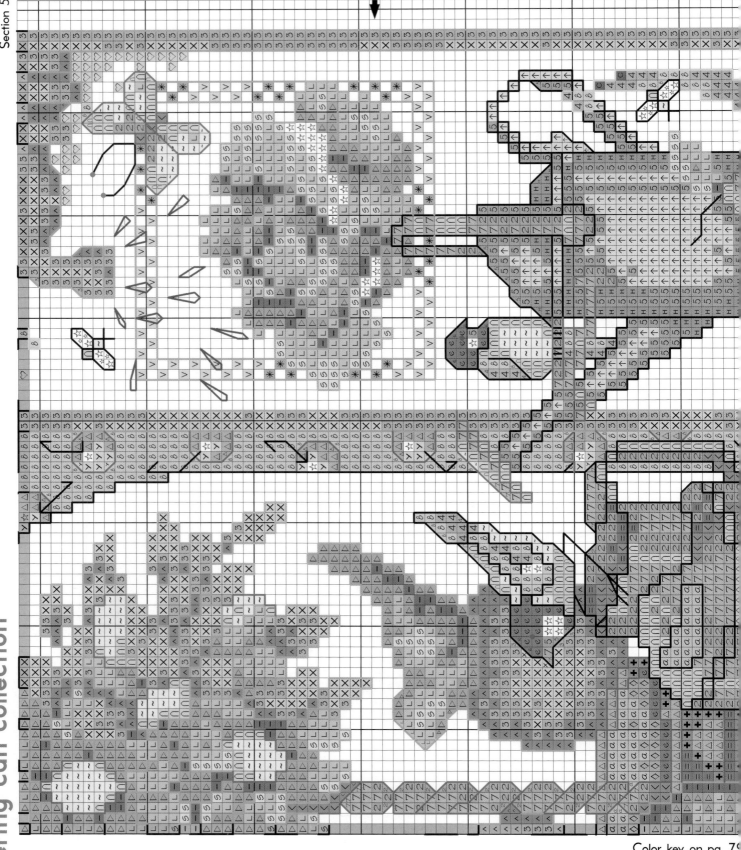

Color key on pg. 79

The Best of Barbara Baatz Hillman

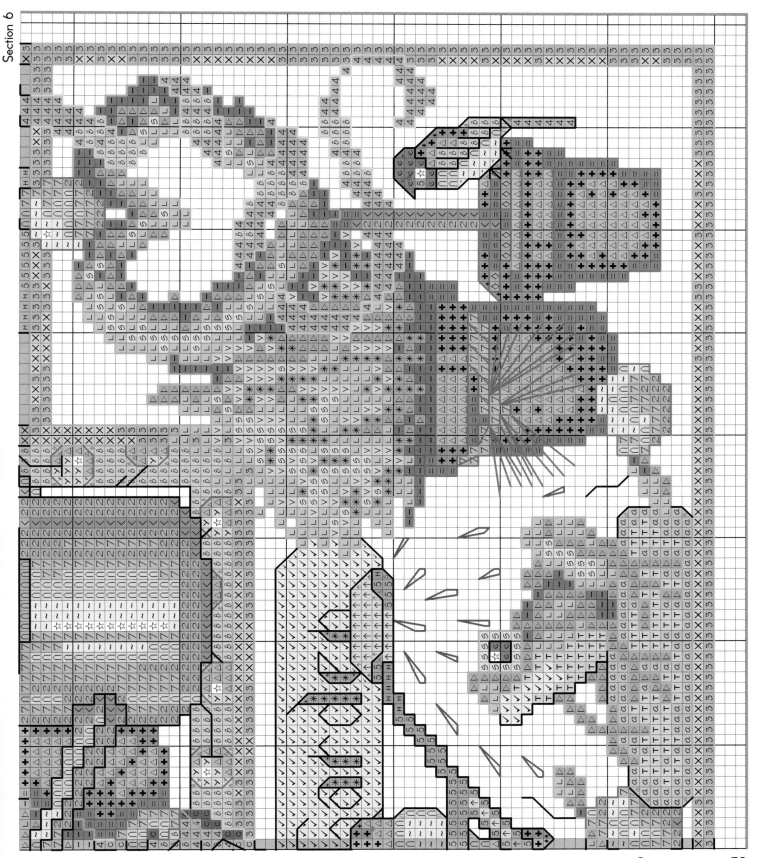

Color key on pg. 79.

X	DMC	1/4X	B'ST
•	blanc		
■	304		
⊘	327		
4	333		
%	340		
P	400	◩	
d	470		
▼	550		◹
+	554		
◗	666		
★	721		
⊠	742	◩	
▽	744	◹	
5	791		◹
$	792		
8	814		◹*

X	DMC	1/4X	B'ST
◆	826		◹
⊠	827		◹
✺	832		
T	834		
✖	898		◹
◉	937		◹
•	976		
2	977	◩	
✳	3350		
Π	3608		
V	3687		
╲	3689		
•	3747		
✔	3777		
•	3799	◨	◹*
=	3821		

Grey area indicates last row of previous section of design.

* Use 814 for apple and 3799 for all other.

The design was stitched over 2 fabric threads on a 45" x 58" piece (standard afghan size) of Ivory All-Cotton Anne Cloth (18 ct).

For afghan, cut off selvages of fabric; measure 5½" from raw edge of fabric and pull out one fabric thread. Fringe fabric up to missing thread. Repeat for each side. Tie an overhand knot at each corner with horizontal and vertical fabric threads. Working from corners use 8 fabric threads for each knot until all threads are knotted.

Refer to Diagram for placement of design on fabric. Use 6 strands of floss for Cross Stitch and 2 for Backstitch.

DIAGRAM

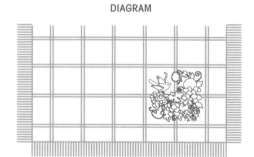

STITCH COUNT (88w x 88h)

14 count	6³⁄₈"	x	6³⁄₈"
16 count	5½"	x	5½"
18 count	5"	x	5"
22 count	4"	x	4"

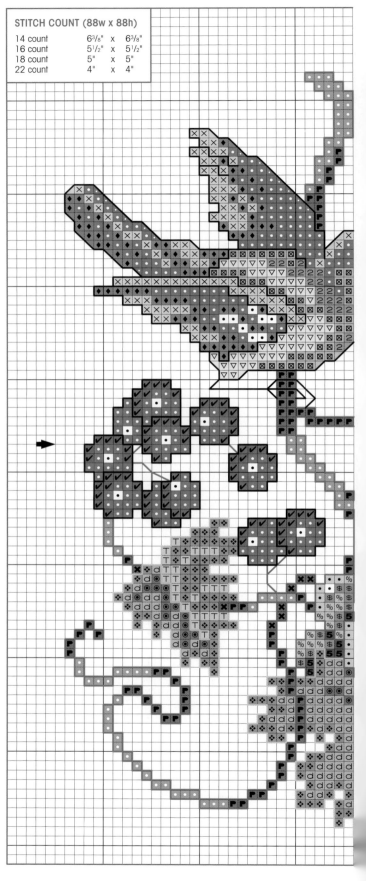

X	DMC	1/4X	B'ST	ANC.	COLOR
•	blanc	•		2	white
▢	310	◣	╱	403	black
◉	326	◣		59	dk rose
✖	349	◣		13	vy dk coral
▢	352	◢		9	coral
V	353			6	lt coral
	434		╱	310	brown
▲	451	◣		233	dk grey
Π	452			232	grey
%	453	◺		231	lt grey
P	500		╱	683	vy dk blue green
❖	603	◣		62	dk pink
•	605	◢		50	pink
T	676			891	dk yellow
♡	745			300	yellow
Ø	815		╱	43	vy dk rose
+	818	▢		23	lt pink
★	946			332	orange
8	3345	◣		268	dk green
✔	3347	◣		266	green
☆	3348			264	lt green
▣	3777			1015	rust
d	3813			875	lt blue green
▢	3815	◣		877	dk blue green
2	3816			876	blue green

▨ Grey area indicates last row of previous section
of design.

Design was stitched over 2 fabric threads on a 13" x11"
piece of White Lugana (25 ct). Three strands of floss
were used for Cross Stitch and 1 for Backstitch. It was
custom framed.

STITCH COUNT (96w x 69h)

14 count	6⁷/₈" x	5"
16 count	6" x	4³/₈"
18 count	5³/₈" x	3⁷/₈"

hummingbird banquet

The Best of Barbara Baatz Hillman

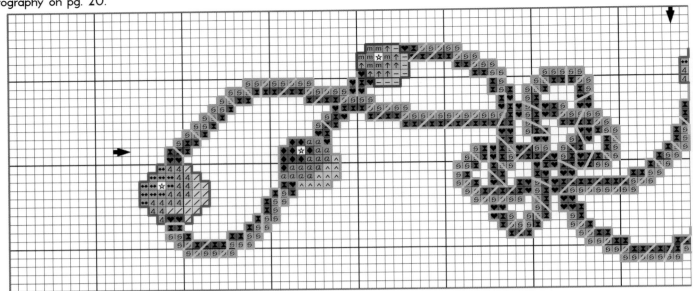

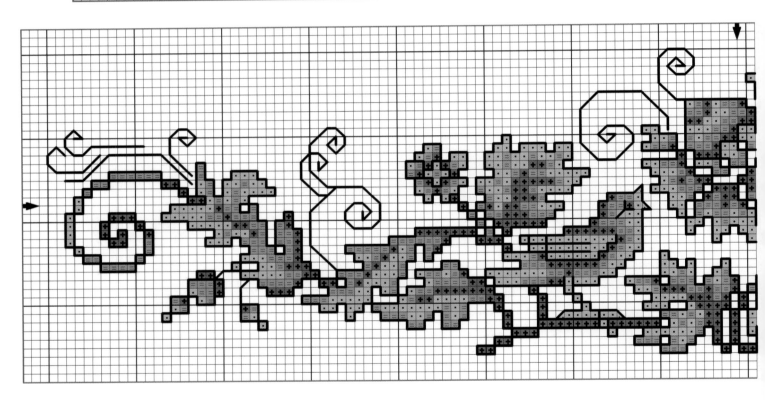

Tassel (122w x 27h)
Blue (158w x 36h)
Pink (158w x 36h)

X	DMC	B'ST	ANC.	COLOR
☆	blanc		2	white
◆	301	/	1049	dk gold
4	597		1064	aqua
/	598		1062	lt aqua
6	610	/	889	brown
m	611		898	khaki
↑	612		832	lt brown

X	DMC	¼X	B'ST	ANC.	COLOR
+	796		/	133	dk blue
=	798			131	blue
•	809	◢		130	lt blue
♥	814		/	45	dk rose
a	976			1001	gold
–	3047			852	lt khaki
S	3687			68	lt rose

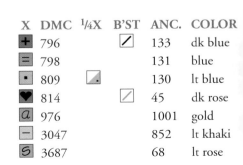

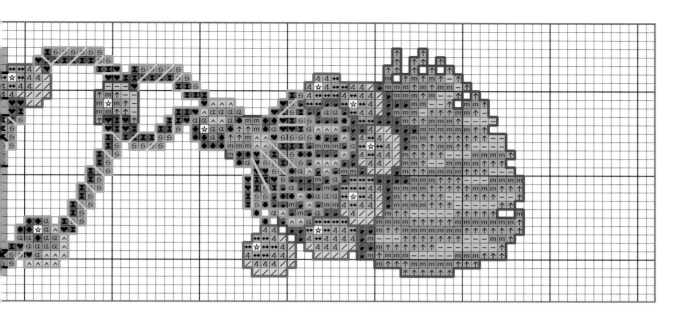

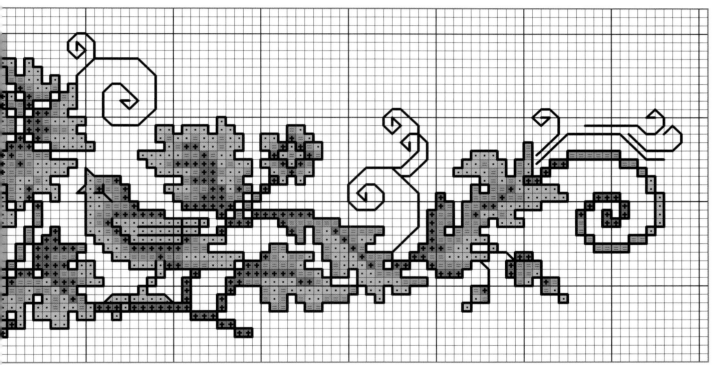

X	DMC	B'ST	ANC.	COLOR
▨	3803		972	rose
✦✦	3809	◪	1066	dk aqua
⌃	3827		311	lt gold
	5282	◪		Gold metallic
▨	Grey area indicates last row of previous section of design.			

stitcher's sampler

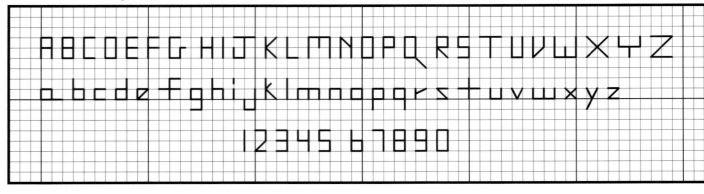

our blessing

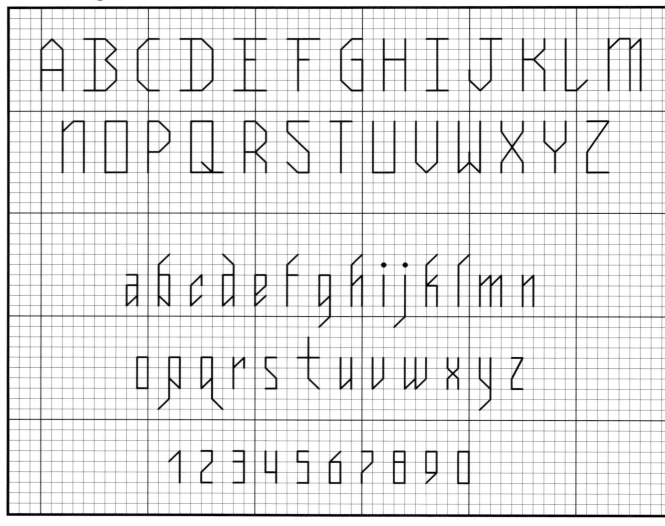

token of love

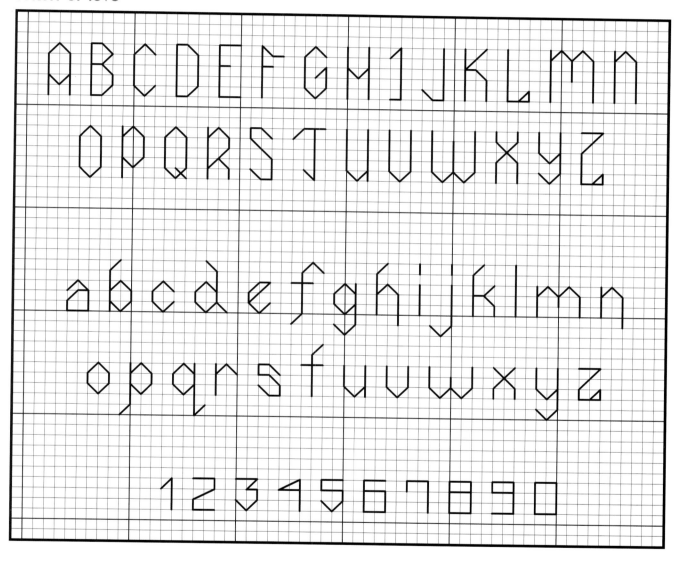

how to read charts

Each chart is made up of a key and a gridded design where each square represents a stitch. The symbols in the key tell which floss color to use for each stitch in the chart. The following headings and symbols are given:

X — Cross Stitch
DMC — DMC color number
¹/₄ X — Quarter Stitch
¹/₂ X — Half Cross Stitch
B'ST — Backstitch
ANC. — Anchor color number
COLOR — the name given to the floss color in this chart

A square filled with a color and a symbol should be worked as a **Cross Stitch** or as a **Half Cross Stitch**.

A triangle with or without a reduced symbol should be worked as a **Quarter Stitch**.

A straight line should be worked as a **Backstitch**.

A large dot listed near the end of the key should be worked as a **French Knot**.

Sometimes the symbol for a **Cross Stitch** may be partially covered when a **Backstitch** crosses the square. Refer to the background color to determine the floss color.

how to stitch

Always work **Cross Stitches**, **Quarter Stitches**, and **Half Cross Stitches** first and then add the **Backstitch** and **French Knots**.

Cross Stitch (X): For horizontal rows, work stitches in two journeys **(Fig. 1)**. For vertical rows, complete each stitch as shown **(Fig. 2)**. When working over two fabric threads, work Cross Stitch as shown in **Fig. 3**.

Fig. 1

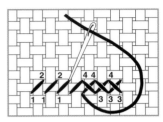

Fig. 2

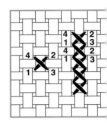

Fig. 3

Quarter Stitch (¹/₄X): Come up at 1 **(Fig. 4)**, then split fabric thread to go down at 2. **Fig. 5** shows the technique for Quarter Stitch when working over two fabric threads.

Fig. 4

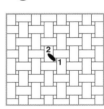

Fig. 5

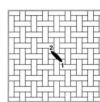

The Best of Barbara Baatz Hillman

PRINTED WITH SOY INK

Made in U.S.A.

Half Cross Stitch (¹/₂X): This stitch is one journey of the Cross Stitch and is worked from lower left to upper right as shown in **Fig. 6**. When working over two fabric threads, work Half Cross Stitch as shown in **Fig. 7**.

Fig. 6

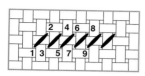

Fig. 7

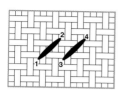

Backstitch (B'ST): For outlines and details, Backstitch should be worked after the design has been completed *(Fig. 8)*. When working over two fabric threads, work Backstitch as shown in **Fig. 9**.

Fig. 8

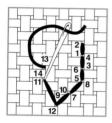

Fig. 9

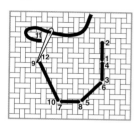

French Knot: Bring needle up at 1. Wrap floss once around needle. Insert needle at 2, tighten knot, and pull needle through fabric, holding floss until it must be released *(Fig. 10)*. For a larger knot, use more floss strands; wrap only once.

Fig. 10

stitching tips

Preparing Fabric
Being sure to allow plenty of margin, cut fabric desired size and overcast raw edges. It is better to waste a little fabric than to come up short after hours of stitching!

Working with Floss
To ensure smoother stitches, separate strands and realign them before threading needle. Keep stitching tension consistent. Begin and end floss by running under several stitches on back; never tie knots.

Dye Lot Variation
It is important to buy all of the floss you need to complete your project from the same dye lot. Although variations in color may be slight when flosses from two different dye lots are held together, the variation is usually apparent on a stitched piece.

Where to Start
The horizontal and vertical centers of each charted design are shown by arrows. You may start at any point on the charted design, but be sure the design will be centered on the fabric. Locate the center of fabric by folding in half, top to bottom and again left to right. On the charted design, count the number of squares (stitches) from the center of the chart to where you wish to start. Then from the fabric's center, find your starting point by counting out the same number of fabric threads (stitches). *(To work over two fabric threads, count out twice the number of fabric threads.)*

Working over Two Fabric Threads
When working over two fabric threads, the stitches should be placed so that vertical fabric threads support each stitch. Make sure that the first Cross Stitch is placed on the fabric with stitch 1-2 beginning and ending where a vertical fabric thread crosses over a horizontal fabric thread *(Fig. 11)*.

Fig. 11

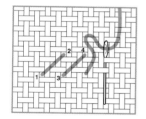

Attaching Beads
To sew bead in place, use one strand of floss and a fine needle that will pass through bead. Secure floss on back of fabric. Bring needle up where indicated on chart, then run needle through bead and down through fabric. To make the bead stand upright, run needle back through bead, making an "X" *(Fig. 12)*. Secure floss on back or move to next bead.

Fig. 12

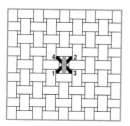

finishing techniques

Floral Fancy Pillow (shown on page 8)

Trim stitched piece to measure 6" x 7". Cut a piece of fabric the same size as stitched piece for backing. For cording, cut one 2" x 32" bias fabric strip, and a 32" length of $^1/_4$" diameter cord. For ruffle, cut one 5" x 64" fabric strip.

For cording, center cord on wrong side of bias fabric strip; matching long edges, fold strip over cord. Using zipper foot, baste along length of strip close to cord; trim seam allowance to $^1/_2$". Matching raw edges and beginning at bottom edge, pin cording to right side of stitched piece, making a $^3/_8$" clip in seam allowance of cording at each corner. Ends of cording should overlap approximately 2"; pin overlapping end out of the way. Starting 2" from beginning end of cording and ending 4" from overlapping end, sew cording to stitched piece. On overlapping end of cording, remove $2^1/_2$" of basting; fold end of fabric back and trim cord so it meets beginning end of cord. Fold end of fabric under $^1/_2$"; wrap fabric over beginning end of cording. Finish basting cording to stitched piece.

For ruffle, press short ends of fabric strip $^1/_2$" to wrong side. Matching wrong sides and long edges, press fabric strip in half. Machine baste $^1/_2$" from raw edges, and gather fabric strip to fit stitched piece. Matching raw edges, pin ruffle to right side of stitched piece, overlapping short ends $^1/_4$". Use a zipper foot and a $^1/_2$" seam allowance to sew ruffle to stitched piece.

Matching right sides and leaving an opening for turning, use a $^1/_2$" seam allowance to sew stitched piece and backing fabric together. Trim seam allowances diagonally at corners; turn pillow right side out carefully pushing corners outward. Stuff pillow with polyester fiberfill and slipstitch opening closed.

Bookmarks (shown on page 6)

For each bookmark, you will need two 4" lengths of $^1/_2$"w lace, a 12" length of $^7/_8$"w ribbon, and fabric glue.

Centering design, trim stitched piece to measure 4" x 8".

On one long edge, turn fabric $^1/_4$" to wrong side and press; turn $^1/_4$" to wrong side again and hem. Repeat for remaining long edge. For remaining raw edges, turn fabric $^1/_4$" to wrong side and press; turn $^1/_4$" to wrong side again and hem. Slipstitch lace to each short edge. Turn raw edges of lace to wrong side and slipstitch in place.

Referring to photo for placement, glue right side of ribbon to wrong side of stitched piece. Trim ends as desired.

Bread Cloth (shown on page 7)

For bread cloth, you will need a 75" length of $^1/_2$"w lace. Press short edges of lace $^1/_2$" to wrong side. Turn each edge of stitched piece $^1/_4$" to wrong side and press; turn $^1/_4$" to wrong side again and hem. Referring to photo, slipstitch straight edge of lace to wrong side of bread cloth.

Table Runner (shown on page 7)

For table runner, you will need two 16" lengths of 2"w lace and two 1" x 16" bias fabric strips.

For trim, fold bias fabric strip in half lengthwise with wrong sides together; press. Matching folded edge of fabric strip to straight edge of lace; baste together. Repeat for remaining fabric strip and lace.

On cross-stitched ends, match right sides and straight edges of trim to raw edge of fabric and use a $^1/_4$" seam allowance to sew trim to right side of fabric. Using a zigzag stitch to prevent fraying, sew close to seam; trim close to zigzag stitch. Press seam allowances to wrong side of table runner. For remaining raw edges, turn fabric $^1/_4$" to wrong side and press; turn $^1/_4$" to wrong side again and hem.

Candle Band (shown on page 7)

For candle band, you will need a 16" length of 2"w lace and two 1" x 16" bias fabric strips.

Centering design, trim stitched piece to measure 16" x $5^1/_2$".

Matching right sides and long edges, fold stitched piece in half. Using a $^1/_4$" seam allowance, sew long edges together; trim seam allowance to $^1/_8$" and turn stitched piece right side out. With seam centered in back, press stitched piece flat.

For trim, fold each bias fabric strip in half lengthwise with wrong sides together; press. For bottom trim, match folded edge of fabric strip to straight edge of lace; baste together.

Referring to photo, topstitch fabric trim to top long edge of stitched piece and fabric and lace trim to bottom long edge of stitched piece. Wrap candle band around candle, turning raw edges to wrong side so that ends meet; slipstitch short ends together.